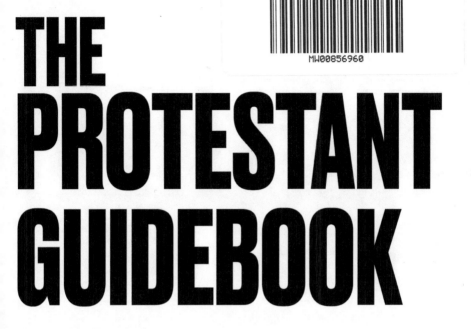

THE PROTESTANT GUIDEBOOK

REIGNITING LUTHER'S LEGACY

BOB WILSON

THE PROTESTANT GUIDEBOOK:
REIGNITING LUTHER'S LEGACY

Copyright 2024

TABLE OF CONTENTS

PREFACE

This book is intended for everyone with an interest in the Protestant faith. When researching a particular faith, it helps to have an independent viewpoint that won't be expressed by most pastors you talk to, most videos you watch, or most news you read.

I was baptized and confirmed Lutheran Protestant. Over the last several decades, I saw a widening disconnect between the teachings of Martin Luther—the founding father of Protestantism—and the teachings of Protestant churches. Exploring this disconnect, I found that the rabbit hole went deeper and deeper. This book is a summary of what I learned from going down that rabbit hole. As someone with a background in research and analysis, I understand the importance of gathering information from a variety of sources, looking at all sides of the subject at hand, and connecting the dots.

In the realm of faith, the gathering of information is made difficult by the heavy censorship that surrounds the subject. This is exacerbated by the timidity of church officials and theologians who think that being politically correct makes them good Christians. The net result of all this is that many of the questions you might wish to ask about Protestantism are considered out of bounds, and any answers you get will be filtered through the lens of political correctness.

The vast majority of authors use mainstream media sources like Wikipedia when conducting research on just about any topic, including religion. I expressly avoided using Wikipedia when writing this book. The fate that has befallen the platform is representative of what has happened to all mainstream media.

Wikipedia co-founder Larry Sanger was recently interviewed by independent journalist Glenn Greenwald. In the interview, Sanger noted that over the past decade or two, Wikipedia has completely lost its objectivity. "No encyclopedia to my knowledge has been as biased as Wikipedia has been . . . It's over the top" said Sanger in the interview.[1]

Sanger added, "We have evidence that the CIA . . . and FBI computers were used to edit Wikipedia." What makes the situation even worse is the complicity of Google, which donated millions of dollars to Wikipedia over the years, further destroying its objectivity.[2]

Wikipedia is a case study in why mainstream media sources are not trustworthy. Most popular media brand names are compromised. They exist not to inform us but to perpetuate the mainstream narrative and control our thinking.

While mainstream sources are fine for topics that aren't politically or culturally sensitive, anyone using them to research faith related topics will be lost before they start. The anti-Christian bias is so extreme that you'll end up with flawed and inaccurate information.

If you buy a best selling book about Protestantism that's printed by a big publisher, you'll encounter the same politically correct, sanitized platitudes that you get on most social media sites. All major publishing houses are part of the mainstream media and should be considered unreliable.

In addition, Google and most major search engines should be considered untrustworthy. Google has been systematically erasing the Internet for the past several years, eliminating content that does not support the Current Thing. By this, I'm referring to mainstream narratives like climate change, overpopulation, etc. that are promoted ad nauseum by the media to disorient and misdirect the public. Google is not so much a search engine anymore, but a concealment engine. It conceals inconvenient truths that do not support the Current Thing.

Christianity has been specifically targeted for censorship by the mainstream media. Discrediting and misrepresenting Christianity is part of an agenda that has existed for several centuries. That agenda will be explored in this book.

The English language itself is becoming increasingly anti-Christian. For hundreds of years, the abbreviations BC and AD were used to delineate dates. Then it was decided that AD should be replaced by CE. This is an attack on Christianity. Many Christian words have also had their meanings twisted. In a later chapter, we'll see how the term 'fundamentalism' has been distorted by the media as part of the anti-Christian agenda.

When given a choice between comfortable lies and uncomfortable truths, we often take the path of comfort. It's tempting to just go along with what the media says and put up with a little cognitive dissonance. I can't promise you that this book will be a comforting read, but I can say with confidence that it will provide you with balanced, unfiltered information that has been sourced from a variety of channels.

I wrote this book because I believe Martin Luther brought something of incomparable value to Christianity when he spearheaded the Reformation half a millennium ago. I also believe that the Protestant faith, in the true form that Luther envisioned, is the purest expression of Christianity in the world today. Sadly, Luther's legacy is in danger of being cancelled.

"AND YE SHALL KNOW THE TRUTH, AND THE TRUTH SHALL MAKE YOU FREE." - JOHN 8:32

The purpose of this book is to give you the true story of Protestantism. The beginning chapters outline the birth of Christianity and the growth of Catholicism in Europe. The next section covers the Protestant Reformation and the Catholic response. Subsequent chapters cover the Jesuit Order and the infiltration of the Protestant Church as well as the fields of education, language and science. This is followed by a look at the current state of the Protestant Church and how it has been compromised by secular trends. The closing chapters discuss the current decline of civilization and show how we can apply the foundational Protestant precept of Sola Scriptura to help navigate our way through what is to come.

By rediscovering the true spirit of the Protestant faith, we can reignite the flame of Martin Luther's legacy. This flame can light the way as we walk the path to cultivating a relationship with God.

1. "Wikipedia Co-Founder Condemns It: Most Biased Encyclopedia in History I SYSTEM UPDATE." Glenn Greenwald. https://www.youtube.com/watch?v=YR6dO8U8okk
2. Ibid.

ΑΩ
EARLY CHRISTIANITY

The trajectory of Christianity has encompassed great successes as well as great failures over the course of its two thousand year history. The first great victory was won by the apostles, who—in the face of severe persecution— were able to spread the Word of God to a critical mass of followers and establish the beginnings of the Christian Church.

This initial success was followed by three centuries of extreme hardship. Christians were forbidden under Roman law to practice their faith and relentlessly persecuted. They were jailed, tortured and executed for their beliefs.

The Roman emperor Constantine converted to Christianity in 312 AD, legalizing its practice and beginning a slow process that would lead to Rome adopting Christianity as its state religion in 380 AD.[1] Although this was in some ways a great step forward for Christianity, Constantine sowed seeds of corruption that would later come to fruition.

Like all politicians, Constantine recognized the importance of making things palatable to the masses. In the case of Christianity, he did this by debasing many key elements of Scripture. One example of this was preserving the Pagan tradition of Sunday worship. This replaced worship on the Sabbath, in violation of the Fourth

Commandment. It later became entrenched as a pillar of Roman Catholicism.

Between the 5th and 11th centuries, Eastern Christian churches under Constantinople developed independently of the Western church under the papacy. Increasing tensions between the two culminated in the Great Schism of 1054, which saw the separation of Christian churches in the East (Orthodox) from those in the West (Catholic).

Backed by the power of Rome, the Roman Catholic Church (RCC) became the undisputed voice of Christianity in the West. It grew into a formidable political powerhouse that could bend the will of nations. Following the same evolutionary path as all expanding organizations, the RCC turned into a bureaucratic behemoth with increasing layers of 'middle management' such as deacons, bishops and cardinals.

Rather than undertaking to freely spread the Word of God to the people of Europe, the RCC hid the Bible in its cathedrals and prevented Christians from seeing it. There was no talk of translating the Bible so the common man would be able to read it. Only a privileged few in the highest ranks of the church were permitted access to Scripture. Pope Gregory IX (1170-1241) declared:

. . . It is forbidden for laymen to read the Old and New Testaments. We forbid them most severely to have the above books in the popular vernacular. The lords of the districts shall carefully seek out the heretics in dwelling, hovels and forests, and even their underground retreats shall be entirely wiped out.[2]

"IT IS EASIER FOR A CAMEL TO GO THROUGH THE EYE OF A NEEDLE, THAN FOR A RICH MAN TO ENTER INTO THE KINGDOM OF GOD." - MATTHEW 19:24

The RCC defended its decision to forbid anyone outside the church to see the Bible by claiming that the common man lacked the ability to interpret Scripture. At least, that was the official reason. The real reason was that if people had the opportunity to see the Bible, they would quickly discern that terms like 'pope' and 'papacy' were nowhere to be found within its pages. Nor would they find terms like 'purgatory' or other Catholic inventions. Much of Catholic doctrine would have been exposed as unbiblical.

By the Middle Ages, the self-serving agenda of the RCC had expanded to include the sale of indulgences, which was set up to finance the expansion of St. Peter's Basilica in Rome. Destitute Christians gave away their last pennies in exchange for a piece of paper from the church that promised the release of a loved one from purgatory or passage to heaven for a sinner. It was quite literally the selling of salvation.

The RCC had unilaterally granted itself the right to perform an action reserved exclusively for God: the power to save souls. The RCC didn't mention to anyone that Scripture is very clear about where this authority rests. Ephesians 2:8 states:

For by grace are ye saved through faith; and that not of yourselves: it is the gift of God:

Without the Bible to guide them, Christians didn't realize that they were wasting their money on worthless pieces of paper. They were not buying salvation, but merely financing the construction of a lavish cathedral.

The selling of indulgences was not the RCC's greatest transgression. It paled in comparison to the church's megalomaniacal plan to bring every European under its clerical rule. To accomplish this, the RCC launched an initiative that would bring decades of terror to Europe.

1. "Constantine's Conversion to Christianity." World History Encyclopedia. https://www.worldhistory.org/article/1737/constantines-conversion-to-christianity/
2. "Bible = 'Hate Speech' spreads to UK." NicholasPOGM. https://www.youtube.com/watch?v=tcgR6Ahg5yc

AΩ
THE INQUISITION

Having enjoyed a millennium-long monopoly on religious practice, the Roman Catholic Church (RCC) was growing increasingly bold in its sectarian domination of Europe by the 1100s. The RCC sought to convert every last European to Catholicism and purge those who resisted. The tyranny of the church was expressed most heinously in multiple campaigns of terror that it waged against the people of Europe in the Middle Ages.

The Inquisition—which was an institution of the RCC encompassing four separate campaigns—involved the judgement of heresy by the RCC with the cooperation of secular authorities. It allowed the RCC to investigate and sentence anyone suspected of not conforming to the beliefs of the RCC. Trials regularly involved the torturing of the accused to extract confessions and reveal the names of other suspected transgressors. Sentences could be carried out in various ways depending on the perceived severity of the heresy, including imprisonment, asset seizure, exile, and execution.

Many have heard of the Spanish Inquisition, a period of terrible bloodshed in medieval Europe that lasted nearly four centuries. That event was actually one of four campaigns that were spearheaded by the RCC:

► Medieval Inquisition (1184-1240)
► Spanish Inquisition (1478-1834)

- Portuguese Inquisition (1536-1821)
- Roman Inquisition (1542-1750)[1]

The New World Encyclopedia notes:

Because of its objective, combating heresy, the Inquisition had jurisdiction only over baptized members of the Church (which, however, encompassed the vast majority of the population). Non-Christians could still be tried for blasphemy by secular courts. Also, most of the witch trials were held by secular courts. The Inquisition could only operate because of the consent of the secular authorities, which recognized the Church's legal jurisdiction in those areas covered by ecclesiastical law, including the right to inflict capital punishment.[2]

It was the cooperation of state powers with the RCC that enabled the unfathomable bloodshed that took place. The RCC exercised an unsurpassed level of legal authority over the lives of Europeans, giving it carte blanche to wage its four campaigns of terror. An infamous quote from Pope Innocent III (1161-1216) provides a good indication of the mindset of the RCC at the time: "Anyone who attempts to construe a personal view of God which conflicts with Church dogma must be burned without pity."[3]

"THEN SAID JESUS UNTO HIM, PUT UP AGAIN THY SWORD INTO HIS PLACE: FOR ALL THEY THAT TAKE THE SWORD SHALL PERISH WITH THE SWORD." - MATTHEW 26:52

The estimates of death counts vary widely. A Spanish secretary named Juan Antonio Llorente (1756–1823) stated in his book *A Critical History of the Inquisition of Spain* that nearly 32,000 were burned at the stake during the Spanish Inquisition, and another 300,000 were put on trial and forced to do penance.[4] Official records didn't track how many prisoners died of torture, disease and maltreatment while serving their sentences, but this number could exceed 100,000 for the Spanish Inquisition alone.[5]

The tyranny of the RCC was not unanimously supported by Catholic clergy. The bloodshed of the Medieval and Spanish Inquisitions, along with corrupt practices like the selling of indulgences, spurred several priests to question the actions of the church.

One such dissenter was John Wycliffe (1328-1384), an English university professor and Catholic priest who made the important contribution of translating the Bible (hitherto available only in Hebrew, Greek and Latin) into English. The translation was completed in the 1380s. Wycliffe was an outspoken critic of the RCC and is credited with being one of the first theologians of his time to declare that Scripture should be the sole source of Christian doctrine.

Following in John Wycliffe's footsteps was William Tyndale (1494-1536), who produced the first printed English New Testament a century and a half after Wycliffe. Aided by the invention of the printing press and Gutenberg's innovation of movable type, Tyndale's Bible was distributed by the thousands. It would later be used in the preparation of the King James Bible, which to this day is regarded as the definitive version of Scripture.

Wycliffe and Tyndale were among the first to see in the actions of the papacy something far worse than any tyranny that had ever descended on Europe. These priests were extremely troubled by the events taking place and turned to Scripture for guidance. Their expert knowledge of the Bible and their skill in interpreting prophecy brought them to a startling but inescapable conclusion: the papacy was the antichrist foretold in the Bible.

This pronouncement was echoed by a vast number of learned clergymen as well as scholars and laymen outside the church. Here is a list of historical figures who denounced the papacy as the antichrist (and the approximate year). Many of these brave individuals paid with their lives for revealing the truth about the papacy:

- Arnulf, Bishop of Orleans (991)
- Gherbert of Rheims (~1000)
- Berenger (11th century)
- Eberhard II, Archbishop of Salzburg (1241)
- Reinerius Saccho, Waldensian (1254)
- Michal of Cesena (~1300)
- John Wycliffe, priest and Oxford University professor (~1360)
- Walter Brute, scholar and associate of John Wycliffe (1391)
- Matthias of Janow (~1381)
- John Purvey, associate of John Wycliffe (~1400)
- Sir John Oldcastle, knight of Hereforedshire and associate of John Wycliffe (~1400)
- William White, associate of John Wycliffe
- Jan Hus, Czech Reformer (~1400)
- Jerome of Prague, Czech Reformer (~1400)
- John Purvey, author and associate of John Wycliffe) (~1390)
- William Tyndale, English Reformer (~1520)
- Huldreich Zwingli, Swiss Reformer (~1520)
- John Calvin (~1550)
- Nicolaus von Amsdorf, associate of Martin Luther (~1550)
- Philipp Melanchthon, German Reformer (~1550)
- Ulriucus Zuinglius, Swiss Reformer

- John à Lasco (1551)
- John Hooper, Bishop of Gloucester (~1550)
- John Bradford, Minister of Christ's Church (~1550)
- Hugh Latimer, Bishop of Worcester (1555)
- Nicholas Ridley, Bishop of London (1555)
- Thomas Cranmer, Archbishop of Canterbury (1556)
- Master Bullingham (1562)
- John Maundrel (1556)
- William Coberly (1556)
- John Spicer (1556)
- Robert Drakes (1556)
- William Tyms (1556)
- Richard Spurge (1556)
- Thomas Spurge (1556)
- John Cavel (1556)
- George Ambrose (1556)
- John Hullie, Minister (1556)
- Henry Adlington (1556)
- Laurence Pernam (1556)
- Henry Wye (1556)
- William Halliwel (1556)
- Thomas Bowyer (1556)
- George Searles (1556)
- Edmund Hurst (1556)
- Lyon Cawch (1556)
- Ralph Jackson (1556)
- John Derifall (1556)
- John Routh (1556)
- Elizabeth Pepper (1556)
- Agnes George (1556)
- Agnes Prest (1557)
- Ralph Allerton (1557)
- James Austoo (1557)
- Margery Austoo (1557)
- Richard Roth (1557)
- John Jewel, Bishop of Salisbury (~1570)
- Matthias Flacius Illyricus, Istrian Reformer (~1575)

- John Knox, Scottish Reformer (~1572)
- Heinrich Bullinger, Pastor, Zurich Cathedral (~1575)
- William Fulke, English Puritan (~1589)
- Georg Nigrinus, Evangelical theologian (~1570)
- John Napier, Scottish Reformer (~1615)[6]

The most famous historical figure who went to battle against the RCC—Martin Luther—also named the papacy as the antichrist. In addition, he went a step further by distributing this knowledge far and wide, as we'll see in the next chapter.

1. "Inquisition." New World Encyclopedia. https://encycloreader.org/db/view.php?id=s3vNtWaL20NW
3. Ibid.
4. "The Horrors of the Church and its Holy Inquisition." Church and State. https://churchandstate.org.uk/2016/04/the-horrors-of-the-church-and-its-holy-inquisition/
5. "What was the death toll during the Inquisition?" Code911, https://code911.top/howto/what-was-the-death-toll-during-the-inquisition#what-was-the-death-toll-during-the-inquisition
6. Wilcoxson, David Nikao. "Revelation Timeline Decoded, Historic Witnesses Against The Antichrist Beast, The Popes Of Rome." https://revelationtimelinedecoded.com/historic-witnesses-against-the-antichrist-beast-the-popes-of-rome/

AΩ

THE BIRTH OF PROTESTANTISM

Martin Luther (1483-1546) was born in Eisleben, Germany, a region that was at the time part of the Roman Empire. As the eldest child, Luther was under pressure from his parents to gain a good education and move up from his roots in the peasantry. His father wanted him to become a lawyer.

Luther struggled with his studies and dropped out of law school to pursue philosophy. He found this equally unsatisfying, believing that the philosophical theories of mere mortals were ultimately flawed due to their subjective nature. He felt that truth could be found only through God, but was unsure how to discover it.

In 1505, Luther experienced an event that changed his life. He was caught in a storm and saw a bolt of lightning hit a nearby tree. Believing he was in grave danger, he cried out, "Saint Anne, help me! I will become a monk!"[1]

Luther kept his vow, and much to the dismay of his father, dropped out of university and entered St. Augustine's Monastery. He took to his duties diligently, believing that Saint Anne had saved his life. Luther regarded himself, and all human beings, as deeply flawed, and had a strong fear of God. He was a man of extreme humility and despite his total dedication to his monastic duties, did not consider himself worthy of God's forgiveness.

Luther thought of God as a cruel and intolerant figure, and he shared these thoughts with his mentor, Johann von Staupitz (1460-1524), expecting to be released from the monastery. Instead, Staupitz encouraged Luther to pursue his doctoral degree. Luther reluctantly agreed, completing his degree in 1512 and taking over Staupitz's position as Chair of the Bible at the University of Wittenberg with his blessing.

Luther had a change of heart regarding the nature of God in 1513, when he came across a passage from Romans 1:17. He wrote:

> Night and day I pondered until I saw the connection between the justice of God and the statement that "the just shall live by his faith." Then I grasped that the justice of God is that righteousness by which through grace and sheer mercy, God justifies us through faith. Thereupon I felt myself to be reborn and to have gone through the open doors into paradise. The whole of Scripture took on a new meaning and, whereas before the "justice of God" had filled me with hate, now it became to me inexpressibly sweet in greater love. This passage of Paul became to me a gate into heaven.[2]

This was a watershed moment for Luther. It transformed his view of God and allowed him to see that it was the divine Word of God—not the church—that would help him resolve his spiritual struggles. This personal revelation demonstrated to Luther the inestimable value of Scripture and the need to keep it at the centre of his faith. It was the seed that would later blossom into Luther's doctrinal philosophy.

The selling of indulgences, which the Roman Catholic Church (RCC) undertook to finance the expansion of St. Peter's Basilica in Rome, came to Luther's attention. He condemned the practice and wrote a list of grievances against the RCC. This list called out the church not only for the selling of indulgences, but several other unscriptural practices. It became known as *The Ninety Five Theses*. It was nailed to the church door in Wittenberg, Germany in 1517, setting off a chain of events that would profoundly alter the course of Christianity.

Luther's act of protest marked the birth of the Reformation. This culminated in the establishment of Protestantism, so named because it protested the unscriptural practices of the RCC.

Luther endured several tribunals at the hands of the RCC. Not only did he stand firm to his convictions, but took advantage of the opportunity to request reforms to the church.

The cornerstone of Luther's faith was Sola Scriptura (Latin for Scripture alone), advocating the Bible as the sole standard of spiritual truth. The tenet of Sola Scriptura is justified by the fact that the Bible is the only work in existence that is inspired by God. II Timothy 3:16-17 states:

All scripture is given by inspiration of God, and is profitable for doctrine, for reproof, for correction, for instruction in righteousness: That the man of God may be perfect thoroughly furnished unto all good works.

Luther stressed that salvation is a gift from God, received through faith rather than works. Ephesians 2:8-9 states:

For by grace are ye saved through faith; and that not of yourselves: it is the gift of God:

Not of works, lest any man should boast.

In addition, he believed that every Christian is able to cultivate a direct relationship with God through Jesus Christ. In the RCC, bishops, cardinals and priests positioned themselves as middlemen which people needed to reach God. Luther knew that this was unbiblical. Proverbs 22:2 states:

> The rich and poor meet together: the Lord is the maker of them all.

Luther's understanding of equality before God can be discerned in his views on Catholic saints. In the RCC, a saint is someone formally recognized by the church as being exceptionally dedicated in their service to God, and includes those believed to have performed miracles and those who have been martyred for their faith. Luther did not believe that any church had the authority to make this judgement. That was something only God could do.

From his *Dris Martini Lutheri Colloquia Mensalia, Or, Dr. Martin Luther's Divine Discourses At His Table, Etc.*, published in 1652, we have Luther's succinct quote: "No great saint lived without errors."[3] This simple truth serves as a reminder that all human beings are fallible. To label one individual as more saintly than another is something none of us is qualified to do.

The RCC refused to entertain any of Luther's recommendations for reform. So desperate was the church to stop Luther that Pope Leo X sent a number of delegations to try to convince him that he was in error.

Luther refused to back down, and in 1520, he was threatened with excommunication. Luther publicly burned the written notice that was given to him in Wittenberg. He was excommunicated in 1521, and was forced to appear at the Diet of Worms, a hearing presided over by Roman

Emperor Charles V. Luther again refused to recant, delivering a famous speech which included the following lines:

> Unless I am convinced by the testimony of the Scriptures or by clear reason (for I do not trust either in the Pope or in the councils alone, since it is well known that they have often erred and contradicted themselves), I am bound by the Scriptures I have quoted and my conscience is captive to the Word of God. I cannot and will not retract anything, since it is neither safe nor right to go against conscience...I cannot do otherwise, here I stand, may God help me. Amen.[4]

Luther was condemned as an outlaw, meaning he could be killed without reprisal. On his way back to Wittenberg, he was abducted by soldiers of Frederick III, disguised as highwaymen to deflect suspicion, and given sanctuary at Frederick's castle in Wartberg.

It was in Wartberg where Luther undertook the monumental task of translating the New Testament into German. For this, he used the second edition of the Greek New Testament prepared by Dutch theologian Desiderius Erasmus (1466-1536). He then oversaw the even greater task of translating the Old Testament with the help of a team of assistants. Luther's translations continued the earlier work of John Wycliffe, who created the first complete translation of the Old and New Testaments into English.[5]

Luther's accomplishments did not end there. Corroborating the suspicions of many of his associates, he identified the antichrist foretold in Scripture as the papacy. In his book *Address to the Christian Nobility of the German Nation Concerning the Reform of the Christian Estate*, published in 1520, Luther declared:

23

It must . . . have been the very prince of devils who said what was written in canon law: "If the pope were so scandalously bad as to lead souls in crowds to the devil, yet he could not be deposed." On this accursed and devilish foundation they build at Rome, and think that we should let all the world go to the devil, rather than resist their knavery. . . . It is to be feared that this is a game of Antichrist or a sign that he is close at hand.[6]

This may come as a surprise if you've been taught (as many of us have) to believe that the antichrist will be a solitary figure appearing in the End Times. As we'll see in a later chapter, this futurist interpretation of Scripture was a disinformation campaign created to take the spotlight off the papacy.

"THEREFORE IF ANY MAN BE IN CHRIST, HE IS A NEW CREATURE: OLD THINGS ARE PASSED AWAY; BEHOLD, ALL THINGS ARE BECOME NEW." - 2 CORINTHIANS 5:17

In 1521, a publication entitled *Passional of Christ and Antichrist* appeared in Wittenberg. This anonymously published satire consisted of 13 two-panel illustrations contrasting scenes from the life of Christ with scenes from the life of the pope. It provides ample evidence supporting the argument that the papacy is the antichrist.

One illustration, for example, bears the title 'The Crown.' It shows Christ crowned with thorns on the left panel and, antithetically, the pope crowned with a tiara of gold on the right. Each illustration reveals the deep contrast between the lives of Christ and the pope to great effect, showing that the pope is the antichrist. It is known that Luther was in contact with the producers of the book, and approved of the publication. However, it is not likely that he actually had a hand in its production.[7]

Luther's writing was more sophisticated than the simple style employed in *Passional of Christ and Antichrist*, and he completed many works. In addition to his translation of the Bible and the many sermons that he wrote, Luther authored doctrinal letters and books including *Lessons on the Epistle of Paul to the Romans*, *On Christian Liberty*, *The Bondage of the Will*, *On Good Deeds*, *Prelude on the Babylonian Captivity of the Church*, *On the Estate of Marriage*, *Large Catechism*, *Small Catechism*, and *Schmalkaldian Articles*.

His polemic writings began with *The Ninety Five Theses* and continued with *The Lecture on Papacy in Rome* and *the Image of Papacy* and *The Judgement on Monastic Vows*. His political writings include *Appeal to the Christian Nobility of the German Nation on Christian State Amendment*, *On Temporal Authority and the Limitations in Obeying It*, *Sermon to the Armies*, *War Against the Turks*, and *The Duty of Civilian Authorities to Oppose Anabaptists with Corporeal Chastisements*.[8]

Luther continued to protest the injustices of the RCC until his dying day. His last and most focused attack against the papacy was *Against the Roman Papacy, An Institution of the Devil*. This work was a response to two letters from Pope Paul III forbidding the emperor from calling a national council to settle religious disputes within the empire. In this publication, Luther denounced the pope as a teacher of lies, blasphemies and idolatries. Luther reiterated his long-held conviction that the papacy was the antichrist and saw it as his duty to expose and refute the transgressions of the RCC so the people would be liberated from its tyranny.[9]

No other human being in history did as much to put the Word of God within the grasp of the common man as Martin Luther did. His accomplishments laid the foundation for a new church that would restore Scripture to its rightful place as the bedrock of Christian faith.

The Reformation had strong political repercussions in Europe, contributing to the dissolution of the Roman Empire and strengthening nationalist ideology throughout the continent. It effectively ended the idea of an international unified Christianity as envisioned by the RCC. Britannica states:

> Protestantism's desire to cultivate literacy and to spread regard for the vernacular served to remove the Latin linguistic bond of older Christendom and to encourage the rise of national boundaries based on languages.[10]

For countries in Europe that embraced Protestantism, religious belief was a new demographic differentiator that separated them from their Catholic neighbours. This promoted patriotism and the strengthening of national identity along religious lines. Protestantism heightened Dutch resistance to the Spanish, and Catholicism heightened Irish resistance to the English.[11]

In hindsight, the spread of the Reformation throughout Europe in the 16th century can be seen as a high point for Christianity on the historical timeline. Liberated from the dogma of the RCC and having access to the Bible in their native language for the first time in history, Christians throughout Europe found a new hope in Protestantism. For a brief time, the future of Christianity looked bright.

The papacy was acutely aware of how the Reformation was impacting its fortunes, and wasted no time in preparing a response. Like all monopolies threatened with a sudden loss in market share, the RCC took decisive action. Pope Paul III approved the creation of the Jesuit Order in 1540. This organization was tasked with stopping the Reformation and hiding the truth that Luther and his contemporaries had discovered about the papacy.

1. "Martin Luther." New World Encyclopedia. https://www.worldhistory.org/Martin_Luther/
2. Ibid.
3. "Martin Luther Quotes About Saints." AZ Quotes. https://www.azquotes.com/author/9142-Martin_Luther/tag/saint
4. "Martin Luther." New World Encyclopedia. https://www.worldhistory.org/Martin_Luther/
5. Textus Receptus Bibles. John Wclifffe Bible 1382. https://textusreceptusbibles.com/Wycliffe
6. Pettibone, Dennis. "Martin Luther's Views on the Antichrist." Journal of the Adventist Theological Society, 18/1 (Spring 2007): 81–100. https://digitalcommons.andrews.edu/cgi/viewcontent.cgi?referer=&httpsredir=1&article=1166&context=jats
7. Wareham, Edmund, Bubenheimer, Ulrich, and Lähnemann, Henrike, editors. *Passional of Christ and Antichrist*. Taylor Institution Library, 2021, pp.xxi-xlvii.
8. "Martin Luther, his written works." Musée protestant. https://museeprotestant.org/en/notice/martin-luther-his-written-works/
9. Pettibone, Dennis. "Martin Luther's Views on the Antichrist." Journal of the Adventist Theological Society, Spring 2007, pp. 97-98.
10. "Protestantism's influence in the modern world." Britannica. https://www.britannica.com/topic/The-Protestant-Heritage/Protestantisms-influence-in-the-modern-world
11. "Nationalism, Modernity, and the Reformation I The Protestant Reformation." Big Site of History. https://bigsiteofhistory.com/nationalism-modernity-and-the-reformation-the-protestant-reformation/

ΑΩ
THE JESUIT ORDER

Just as the oligarchs of each nation have their own extrajudicial private army—the CIA in the U.S., MI6 in the UK, etc.—to protect their interests, the Roman Catholic Church (RCC) has theirs. It's called the Jesuit Order.

Anyone who has grown up watching Hollywood movies probably has a very positive view of the Jesuits. They're typically portrayed as noble priests who travelled to distant lands to establish missions and convert the native peoples to Christianity. This perception is fuelled by films like *The Mission* (dir. Roland Joffé, 1986). This movie tells the story of 18th century Spanish Jesuits protecting a South American tribe from falling under the rule of pro-slavery Portugal.[1]

Jesuit priests have indeed undertaken roles similar to what is shown in movies like *The Mission*. However, these missionaries are merely the proverbial tip of the iceberg of the Jesuit Order. They're essentially the public relations officers of the order who are made visible to the public eye. Much in the same way that kingpins of organized crime occasionally drop a few million at their favourite charity, the Jesuits have always understood the importance of maintaining appearances. To understand the real mission of the Jesuit Order, we have to go back to its beginnings half a millennium ago.

Don Inigo Lopez de Recalde was born in the Spanish province of Guipuzcoa in 1491. His parents were wealthy Marranos and historians believe he was either a crypto-Jew (someone who is outwardly Christian but secretly practises Judaism) or a philo-Semite. Progressing from pageboy to courtier and finally soldier, the unruly and conceited youth suffered a severe leg wound in battle that left him with a permanent limp. His failure to fully recover from this traumatic experience resulted in a nervous breakdown.[2]

While recovering from his injury, Don Inigo acquainted himself with the Catholic faith, reading various books about the life of Christ and Roman Catholic saints. He was reported to have many feverish visions that revealed to him the mysteries of Catholic doctrine. Some historians, such as Edmond Paris, believe that he had a nervous disorder that predisposed him to hallucinations. He romanized his name and became known as Ignatius of Loyola.[3]

Ignatius formed the Jesuit Order (which he blasphemously named the Society of Jesus) in 1534, when he was 44 years old. Loyola's cofounders—Alfonso Salmeron, Diego Lainez, Nicolas Bodadilla, and Simao Rodriguez—were thought to be Marrano Jews.[4] In his book *The Jesuit Order as a Synagogue of Jews*, Robert Aleksander Maryks notes that the Jesuit Order was financially backed by the crypto-Jewish community of Spain.

It was not until 1540 that the organization's constitution was approved in Rome by Pope Paul III. Ignatius and his fellow Jesuits pledged their unconditional assistance to the pope and slowly wormed their way into his favour.

The Jesuit Order was set up as a military organization, with all members reporting to the Superior General. Ignatius was the first Superior General (also referred to as the Black Pope, because he operated out of public view). There are various types of Jesuit members, including priests, brothers, and coadjutors. Having a variety of pieces on the chess board gives the Jesuit Order tactical flexibility.

The formation of a Jesuit priest or brother is a lengthy process that can last more than fifteen years. Coadjutors, who are the secular allies of the Jesuits, serve to promote the Jesuit agenda at every level. They include ordinary salary and wage earners as well as leaders in industry, banking and the media. The existence of these coadjutors confirms that the Jesuit agenda goes beyond missionary work.

Every Jesuit takes an oath when joining the Order, in which a promise of poverty, chastity and obedience is given. After reaching a certain level, a second oath is taken, known as the Jesuit extreme oath of induction. This oath reads like a declaration of war. It is reproduced here in its entirety:

THE JESUIT OATH

I now, in the presence of Almighty God, the Blessed Virgin Mary, the blessed Michael the Archangel, the blessed St. John the Baptist, the holy Apostles St. Peter and St. Paul and all the saints and sacred hosts of heaven, and to you, my ghostly father, the Superior General of the Society of Jesus, founded by St. Ignatius Loyola in the Pontificate of Paul the Third, and continued to the present, do by the womb of the virgin, the matrix of God, and the rod of Jesus Christ, declare and swear, that his holiness the Pope is Christ's Vice-regent and is the true and only head of the Catholic or

Universal Church throughout the earth; and that by virtue of the keys of binding and loosing, given to his Holiness by my Savior, Jesus Christ, he hath power to depose heretical kings, princes, states, commonwealths and governments, all being illegal without his sacred confirmation and that they may safely be destroyed.

Therefore, to the utmost of my power I shall and will defend this doctrine of his Holiness' right and custom against all usurpers of the heretical or Protestant authority whatever, especially the Lutheran of Germany, Holland, Denmark, Sweden, Norway, and the now pretended authority and churches of England and Scotland, and branches of the same now established in Ireland and on the Continent of America and elsewhere; and all adherents in regard that they be usurped and heretical, opposing the sacred Mother Church of Rome. I do now renounce and disown any allegiance as due to any heretical king, prince or state named Protestants or Liberals, or obedience to any of the laws, magistrates or officers.

I do further declare that the doctrine of the churches of England and Scotland, of the Calvinists, Huguenots and others of the name Protestants or Liberals to be damnable and they themselves damned who will not forsake the same.

I do further declare, that I will help, assist, and advise all or any of his Holiness' agents in any place wherever I shall be, in Switzerland, Germany, Holland, Denmark, Sweden, Norway, England, Ireland or America, or in any other Kingdom or territory I shall come to, and do my uttermost to extirpate the heretical Protestants or Liberals' doctrines and to destroy all their pretended powers, regal or otherwise.

I do further promise and declare, that notwithstanding I am dispensed with, to assume my religion heretical, for the propaganda of the Mother Church's interest, to keep secret and private all her agents' counsels from time to time, as they may entrust me and not to divulge, directly or indirectly, by word, writing or circumstance whatever; but to execute all that shall be proposed, given in charge or discovered unto me, by you, my ghostly father, or any of this sacred covenant.

I do further promise and declare, that I will have no opinion or will of my own, or any mental reservation whatever, even as a corpse or cadaver (perinde accadaver), but will unhesitatingly obey each and every command that I may receive from my superiors in the Militia of the Pope and of Jesus Christ.

That I may go to any part of the world withersoever I may be sent, to the frozen regions of the North, the burning sands of the desert of Africa, or the jungles of India, to the centers of civilization of Europe, or to the wild haunts of the barbarous savages of America, without murmuring or repining, and will be submissive in all things whatsoever communicated to me.

I furthermore promise and declare that I will, when opportunity present, make and wage relentless war, secretly or openly, against all heretics, Protestants and Liberals, as I am directed to do, to extirpate and exterminate them from the face of the whole earth; and that I will spare neither age, sex or condition; and that I will hang, waste, boil, flay, strangle and bury alive these infamous heretics, rip up the stomachs and wombs of their women and crush their infants' heads against the walls, in order to annihilate forever their execrable race.

That when the same cannot be done openly, I will secretly use the poisoned cup, the strangulating cord, the steel of the poniard or the leaden bullet, regardless of the honor, rank, dignity, or authority of the person or persons, whatever may be their condition in life, either public or private, as I at any time may be directed so to do by any agent of the Pope or Superior of the Brotherhood of the Holy Faith, of the Society of Jesus.

In confirmation of which, I hereby dedicate my life, my soul and all my corporal powers, and with this dagger which I now receive, I will subscribe my name written in my own blood, in testimony thereof; and should I prove false or weaken in my determination, may my brethren and fellow soldiers of the Militia of the Pope cut off my hands and my feet, and my throat from ear to ear, my belly opened and sulphur burned therein, with all the punishment that can be inflicted upon me on earth and my soul be tortured by demons in an eternal hell forever!

All of which, I do swear by the Blessed Trinity and blessed Sacraments, which I am now to receive, to perform and on my part to keep inviolable; and do call all the heavenly and glorious host of heaven to witness the blessed Sacrament of the Eucharist, and witness the same further with my name written and with the point of this dagger dipped in my own blood and sealed in the face of this holy covenant."[5]

The Jesuit modus operandi is to turn each of its members into the ultimate soldier—one who obeys commands unconditionally and would gladly die for the Jesuit cause. Many military organizations, including Heinrich Himmler's S.S. and the U.S. Marines, are believed to have modelled themselves on the Jesuit Order.

Pope Paul III's papacy began in 1534 and lasted until 1549. He was confronted with the greatest threat the RCC had faced in its entire history: the Protestant Reformation. He responded by approving the creation of the Jesuit Order in 1540, launching the Roman Inquisition in 1542, and convening the Council of Trent in 1545.

The Roman Inquisition was a brutal and merciless campaign of terror. The streets of Europe ran red with the blood of Protestants. One of the most horrific events of this period was The St. Bartholomew Day Massacre of 1572.

The prolonged slaughter actually lasted over two months, during which some 50,000 Huguenots (French Protestants) were massacred in Paris.[6]

A number of wars broke out as the RCC, backed by Catholic governments, tried to stop the spread of Protestantism. These included the Wars of Religion in France (1562-1598) and the Dutch Revolt (1565 -1648).

The Roman Inquisition also became the precursor to the devastating Thirty Years' War (1618-1648) that eventually cost Europe nearly half its population. Estimates of the death toll from all inquisitions combined range from 600,000 to the millions.[7]

The Council of Trent was convened in 1545 and met intermittently until 1563. It enacted the formal Roman Catholic reply to the doctrinal challenges of the Protestant Reformation.[8]

When I began researching the Council of Trent, I assumed that it was intended to create a dialogue between Catholics and Protestants. Protestants were in fact invited to participate, but on the condition that they had no right to vote on any decisions. Not surprisingly, no Protestants attended.[9] This begs the question, why bother convening such a council at all? It had all the makings of a pointless exercise in bureaucracy. However, we'll see later that there was one significant outcome, which appears to have been quite accidental.

Here are a few of the official conclusions that the RCC reached during the Council of Trent:

► Anyone who believes that salvation can be attained outside the RCC is accursed.

- ▶ Anyone who believes in justification by grace through faith is accursed.
- ▶ Anyone who does not believe that the pope is the vicar of Christ is accursed.
- ▶ No man has the right to choose his own religion.
- ▶ No man has the right to publish what he feels is the truth.
- ▶ No man has the right to freedom of conscience.[10]

These conclusions were not new, but merely reaffirmed the church's position on these issues.

Ignatius of Loyola sent two Jesuits, Lainez and Salmeron, to act as key participants in the council sessions. They were supposedly brought in to argue RCC doctrine, and historians like to praise their brilliant debating skills. However, since no Protestants were present, it remains a mystery who they were debating against.

Historians claim that the Council of Trent resulted in sweeping reforms to the RCC, but the extent of these reforms has been greatly exaggerated. The website SimplyCatholic admits that "Trent did not end the practice of indulgences. No changes were made to Catholic teaching as a result of the Council." It also states that a few administrative changes were made to the running of the church:

- ▶ Bishops were allowed control of only one diocese at a time, rather than several.
- ▶ Jurisdiction of monasteries was placed under bishops rather than the pope.
- ▶ It was required that a seminary be established in every diocese.[11]

To summarize, the Council of Trent was not the milestone in Catholic reform that historians make it out to be. It was an echo chamber in which Catholics who believed the RCC was the one true church argued their position to other Catholics who believed the RCC was the one true church. After nearly two decades of deliberations, the parties involved concluded that the RCC was the one true church. No concessions to the Reformation were made, and only a few minor administrative changes were implemented with respect to the running of the church.

There was one important outcome of the Council of Trent that was not part of its official mandate. We come now to a major operation undertaken by the Jesuit Order in its counterattack against the Reformation. This operation has been in play for nearly 500 years, and its effects are still felt to this day.

A Jesuit priest by the name of Francisco Ribera formulated a new interpretation of Scripture that would discredit a charge that had been made against the papacy. Martin Luther declared that the papacy was none other than the antichrist. Luther was not the first to make this declaration. As we saw earlier, many leading religious figures had made the same assertion prior to Luther, and dozens more supported it when the Reformation was in full swing.

In 1590, Ribera published a commentary on the Book of Revelation in which he posited that the antichrist was not the papacy, but a single individual who would appear at some point in the future. We know that Ribera's claim is false since 1 John 2:18 states:

Little children, it is the last time: and as ye have heard that antichrist shall come, even now are there many antichrists; whereby we know that it is the last time.

It's clear from this verse that the antichrist is not a single individual. There are multiple antichrists.

Ribera's bit of misdirection conveniently took the spotlight off the papacy. Bending Scripture to the RCC agenda, Ribera introduced the futurist interpretation of prophecy. This later became a cornerstone of dispensationalism, a false interpretation of Scripture popularized by John Nelson Darby (1800-1882).

Dispensationalists believe that there will be a future seven year tribulation which will see the coming of the antichrist in the form of a single individual. They also believe that a pre-tribulation rapture will rescue Christians from the calamitous tribulation period before it begins.

"AND IF ANY MAN SHALL TAKE AWAY FROM THE WORDS OF THE BOOK OF THIS PROPHECY, GOD SHALL TAKE AWAY HIS PART OUT OF THE BOOK OF LIFE, AND OUT OF THE HOLY CITY, AND FROM THE THINGS WHICH ARE WRITTEN IN THIS BOOK." - REVELATION 22:19

At the time of its publication, Ribera's futurist interpretation of prophecy didn't have any immediate impact on the widely held view that the papacy was the antichrist. However, over the next few hundred years, the Jesuits methodically promoted the futurist deception at every opportunity. It became infused in popular culture, the mainstream media, and even Bible colleges. In retrospect, it was one of the greatest public relations victories in the history of the Catholic Church.[12]

To this day, Ribera's futurism remains the dominant interpretation of Revelation. It is the interpretation favoured by the mainstream media. Hollywood movies like *Rosemary's Baby* (dir. Roman Polanski, 1968), *The Omen* (dir. Richard Donner, 1976) and *The Devil's Advocate* (dir. Taylor Hackford, 1997) peddle the fiction of a future antichrist.

Type 'antichrist' in the YouTube search box and you won't find a single video mentioning the papacy. The same search on Google is equally futile. The Jesuits have done a thorough job of spreading the lie of futurism and preventing people from seeing the truth.

American lawyer turned pastor Cyrus Scofield published the Scofield Reference Bible in 1909. This work is based on the text of the King James Bible, but adds hundreds of footnotes which put a futurist spin on the Seventy Weeks of Daniel and the Book of Revelation. In the Scofield Reference Bible, these passages are re-imagined to foretell the arrival of the antichrist in the form of a single individual in the End Times.[13]

The Moody Bible Institute of Chicago, Illinois, founded in 1886, was one of the earliest proponents of dispensationalist theory in the U.S. and had close ties to Scofield. In fact, Scofield started a Bible Correspondence Course in 1890 which was taken over by the Moody Bible Institute in 1914.[14]

On the heels of Moody, two associates of Scofield, Lewis Sperry Chafer (1871-1952) and William Henry Griffith Thomas (1861-1924), founded the Dallas Theological Seminary in 1924. Students of this seminary and many others used the Scofield Reference Bible and were taught the futurist deception. When these students graduated and formed their ministries, the deception was spread throughout the U.S.:

> The Scofield Study Bible was received by Congregationalists, Baptists, and some Presbyterian denominations. Through the immensely popular Scofield Study Bible, dispensationalism became the standard for biblical interpretation among traditional Southern Baptists in the early twentieth century.[15]

The futurist deception was not the only fiction perpetrated by the Scofield Reference Bible. The Zionist movement, which had its beginnings in the latter half of the 19th century, co-opted Scofield to promote the quest for a Jewish homeland. Some historians argue that Scofield was under Zionist control from the beginning.

Jewish attorney Samuel Untermyer was a prominent Zionist who bent the rules to admit Scofield into the Lotus Club, an exclusive New York men's club, in 1901. Untermeyer introduced Scofield to several key Zionist leaders, including Samuel Gompers, Fiorello LaGuardia, Abraham Straus, Bernard Baruch and Jacob Schiff. As a failed lawyer with a criminal record, Scofield would have had no hope of getting into the Lotus Club without Untermyer's help. This suggests that Untermyer was using Scofield as an unwitting pawn, and that the Scofield Reference Bible was in fact Untermyer's brainchild—the Trojan Horse that he would unleash on American Christians.[16]

In his copious footnotes, Scofield falsely equated the biblical Israel of the Old Testament with the not yet created modern state of Israel. The takeaway from this misreading of Scripture was that the plan to create the modern state of Israel was divinely sanctioned.

As a bestseller, the Scofield Reference Bible duped millions of Christians across the U.S. into supporting Zionism. It had already been in print for nearly half a century when the state of Israel was created on annexed Palestinian land in 1948. Thanks to Scofield, many American Christians did not see this event as a violation of international law, but as the will of God.[17]

In his YouTube video "Is Israel Fulfilling End Times Prophecy?" Greg Sereda of Bible Flock Box notes that it is faith in Jesus Christ that makes someone an Israelite in the eyes of God. The name Israel (which translates as One Who Struggles With God) first appears in the Old Testament in Genesis 32:28, when God declares to Jacob —a man who had persevered in the face of adversity—that he will no longer be known as Jacob, but as Israel. This affirmation was what Jacob had been yearning to hear his entire life, and was a watershed moment for him. Thus an Israelite can be defined as someone who experiences the trials and tribulations of learning to be a Christian.[18]

The true meanings of the terms Israel and Israelite have been lost in the maelstrom of contemporary geopolitical discourse. For those familiar with Scripture, it's obvious that these terms have been subverted and politicized to further the Zionist cause. Few realize that the modern meanings of these words have nothing to do with their biblical counterparts.

American Christians continue to support Zionism to this day, unaware that the modern state of Israel and its inhabitants have no connection to the Israel of the Bible. They have therefore turned a blind eye to the Palestinian genocide that has been taking place in the Middle East for nearly a century, on the false grounds that Israel and its people are somehow special in the eyes of God.

The latest and most devastating escalation of Israeli aggression began in October 2023. The civilian death toll in Gaza reached such a level that dozens of governments rebuked Israel and demanded that its government be held accountable for war crimes. Many of these governments do not preside over Christian peoples, yet they have the ability to recognize the evil that millions of American Christians pardon due to their misunderstanding of Scripture.

Let's return now to the Jesuit Order. We covered Francisco Ribera's futurist deception earlier in this chapter. This was one of many tactics the Jesuits employed to quench the flame of the Reformation. As we'll see in subsequent chapters, the Jesuit agenda encompassed not only the infiltration of the Protestant Church, but the education system, the English language, and several fields of science as well. These schemes were orchestrated covertly and the Jesuits were often able to avoid being exposed.

The Jesuit Order's predilection for meddling in the politics of its host countries was its Achilles' heel. By the 18th century, many governments had uncovered Jesuit schemes aimed at manipulating their domestic affairs. They took decisive action. The governments of Portugal and France were among the first to expel the Jesuit Order from their countries. Several other European states followed suit.

In response to cries against the infamy of the Jesuit Order throughout Europe, Pope Clement XIV (1705-1774) officially dissolved the order in 1773. Clement refused to condemn the Jesuits, euphemistically noting that he was merely making an administrative adjustment in the interests of the church. The suppression was a blow to the RCC, and many schools were closed. However, the Jesuits didn't disappear completely. They just went underground. A few decades later, in 1814, the order was restored.[19]

The Jesuit Order embarked on a decades long project to rebuild itself. It has since grown into a global organization with considerable manpower and resources. When Edmond Paris wrote *The Secret History of the Jesuits* in 1983, he estimated that there were some 33,000 official members of the Jesuit Order globally—in the author's words, "a truly secret army containing in its ranks heads of political parties, high ranking officials, generals, magistrates, physicians, faculty professors, etc."[20]

Although their operations are carried out covertly, they have frequently been exposed. As a result, the Jesuits were expelled from 83 countries, city states and cities, for engaging in political infiltration and subversion plots, between 1555 and 1931.[21]

Even today, governments are continuing their crackdown against Jesuit iniquity. In 2023, Nicaragua cancelled the legal status of the Jesuit Order and ordered its assets confiscated.[22]

The Jesuits do not carry out all their operations independently. They have assistance from two organizations that are frequently complicit in their schemes: the Illuminati and the freemasons.

1. "The Mission." IMDB. https://www.imdb.com/title/tt0091530/
2. Paris, Edmond. *The Secret History of the Jesuits*. Ontario, CA: Chick Publications, 1983, p.22.
3. Ibid.
4. "Jews Control the Jesuits." The World We Live In. https://luis46pr.wordpress.com/2018/04/16/jews-control-the-jesuits/
5. Jesuit Extreme Oath of Induction. https://www.reformation.org/jesuit-oath.html

6. "The Jesuit Antichrist Arrives." Earthling. https://earthlinggb.wordpress.com/2011/04/06/jesuits/
7. "The Horrors of the Church and its Holy Inquisition." https://bibliotecapleyades.net/vatican/esp_vatican29.htm
8. "Counter-Reformation." Britannica. https://www.britannica.com/event/Counter-Reformation
9. Mark, Joshua J. "Council of Trent." World History Encyclopedia, June 16, 2022. https://www.worldhistory.org/Council_of_Trent/
10. Arendt, James. "The Reason for Eroded Civil Liberties: The Edicts of the Council of Trent." August 24, 2022, https://www.jamesjpn.net/government/the-heart-of-the-evils-of-the-world-edicts-of-the-council-of-trent/
11. Emmons, D.D. "Myths and Facts about the Council of Trent." Simply Catholic. https://www.simplycatholic.com/myths-and-facts-about-the-council-of-trent/
12. Nachtigal, Yvonne. "The Purpose and Origins of Futurism." Christian Observer, May 4, 2016. https://christianobserver.net/the-purpose-and-origins-of-futurism/
13. Wilcoxson, David Nikao. "Jesuit End Times Antichrist Deception." End Time Deceptions. https://christianitybeliefs.org/end-times-deceptions/jesuit-end-times-antichrist-deception/
14. "The Terrible Error of the Scofield Bible." Fellowship of God's Covenant People. https://fgcp.org/content/terrible-error-scofield-bible
15. Wilcoxson, David Nikao. "Jesuit End Times Antichrist Deception." End Time Deceptions. https://christianitybeliefs.org/end-times-deceptions/jesuit-end-times-antichrist-deception/
16. "Putting on Sheep's Clothing: The Other Man Behind Scofield." http://archive.constantcontact.com/fs086/1103027403968/archive/1110577242208.html
17. "How the Scofield Bible turned Christians into Zionists." Odysee. https://odysee.com/@thisworldworks:1/OJ9jVPlfvjF9:b
18. "Is Israel Fulfilling End Times Prophecy?" YouTube. https://www.youtube.com/watch?v=2x5oik1PzC8
19. "Jesuit Order Temporarily Dissolved." Christianity.com. https://www.christianity.com/church/church-history/timeline/1701-1800/jesuit-order-temporarily-dissolved-11630286.html
20. Paris, Edmond. *The Secret History of the Jesuits*. Ontario, CA: Chick Publications, 1983, p.41.
21. Shepherd, J.E.C. *The Babington Plot: Jesuit Intrigue in Elizabethan England*. Wittenburg Publications, 1987.

22. "Nicaragua cancels legal status of Catholic Jesuit order." Reuters, August 23, 2023. https://www.reuters.com/world/americas/nicaragua-cancels-legal-status-catholic-jesuit-order-2023-08-23/

ΑΩ
THE ILLUMINATI

The Jesuit Order works in cooperation with other organizations to achieve its objectives. The Illuminati are one such organization. Consulting ten different historians will give you ten different versions of who the Illuminati are and how they originated. The vast majority of recently written accounts of the Illuminati from mainstream sources are heavily redacted and have glaring omissions. There's a popular misconception that Bavarian lawyer Adam Weishaupt (1748-1830) founded the Illuminati in 1776. The movement actually originated long before that.

Far-reaching independent journalism did not exist prior to the Internet. Information was disseminated exclusively through books, newspapers, radio and television, which means it was strictly controlled. No independent writers or journalists (who were interested in spreading the truth as opposed to getting paid to peddle their employer's narratives) existed, save for a few intrepid souls distributing flyers in their neighbourhoods and selling handmade books at the local flea market.

Fortunately, encyclopedias have been around for over a century, and early editions can still be found that have not been censored. The 11th edition of Britannica dates from 1911 and offers a fairly complete account of the Illuminati. Key points of the entry are reproduced here (paragraph breaks have been added for readability):

Illuminati (Lat. illuminare), a designation in use from the 15th century, and applied to, or assumed by, enthusiasts of types distinct from each other, according as the "light" claimed was viewed as directly communicated from a higher source, or as due to a clarified and exalted condition of the human intelligence.

To the former class belong the alumbrados of Spain. Menendez Pelayo first finds the name about 1492 (in the form aluminados, 1498), but traces them back to a Gnostic origin, and thinks their views were promoted in Spain through influences from Italy. . .

Ignatius Loyola, while studying at Salamanca (1527) was brought before an ecclesiastical commission on a charge of sympathy with the alumbrados, but escaped with an admonition. Others were not so fortunate. In 1529 a congregation of unlettered adherents at Toledo was visited with scourging and imprisonment. Greater rigours followed, and for about a century the alumbrados afforded many victims to the Inquisition, especially at Cordova.

The movement (under the name of Illuminés) seems to have reached France from Seville in 1623, and attained some proportions in Picardy when joined (1634) by Pierre Guérin, curé of Saint-Georges de Roye, whose followers, known as Guérinets, were suppressed in 1635 (Hermant, Hist. des hérésies, 1717). . .

A short-lived movement of republican freethought, to whose adherents the name Illuminati was given, was founded on May-day 1776 by Adam Weishaupt (d. 1830), professor of Canon Law at Ingolstadt, an ex-Jesuit. The chosen title of this Order or Society was Perfectibilists (Perfektibilisten). Its members, pledged to obedience to their superiors, were divided into three main classes;

the first including "novices," "minervals" and "lesser illuminati"; the second consisting of freemasons, "ordinary," "Scottish" and "Scottish knights"; the third or "mystery" class comprising two grades of "priest" and "regent" and of "magus" and "king."

Relations with masonic lodges were established at Munich and Freising in 1780. The order had its branches in most countries of the European continent, but its total numbers never seem to have exceeded two thousand. The scheme had its attraction for literary men, such as Goethe and Herder, and even for the reigning dukes of Gotha and Weimar. Internal rupture preceded its downfall, which was effected by an edict of the Bavarian government in 1785. Later, the title Illuminati was given to the French Martinists, founded in 1754 by Martinez Pasqualis, and to their imitators, the Russian Martinists, headed about 1790 by Professor Schwartz of Moscow; both were Cabalists and allegorists, imbibing ideas from Jakob Boehme and Emmanuel Swedenborg (Bergier, Dict. de théol.).[1]

This entry corroborates several other sources that reference the alumbrados of Spain as the originators of the Illuminati, noting their ties with Ignatius of Loyola. The alumbrados were in many ways similar to Loyola's Jesuits, in that they were organized as a secret society with religious elements and sought influence over world events. The key difference was that the Illuminati did not have the support of the Catholic Church, and because of this, they were initially punished as heretics during the inquisitions.

What appears to have happened is that Ignatius of Loyola, who was already involved with the Illuminati when he started the Jesuit Order, subsumed the Illuminati under the Jesuits. The Britannica entry identifies Adam

Weishaupt as an ex-Jesuit, which strengthens this hypothesis.

What is missing from the Britannica entry is any mention of the Illuminati's mandate, suggesting that it was not sufficiently palatable for printing. If the organization was just a harmless networking group for businessmen and merchants, Britannica would have stated that.

"AND HAVE NO FELLOWSHIP WITH THE UNFRUITFUL WORKS OF DARKNESS, BUT RATHER REPROVE THEM. FOR IT IS A SHAME EVEN TO SPEAK OF THOSE THINGS WHICH ARE DONE OF THEM IN SECRET." - EPHESIANS 5:11-12

Some historians studying the Illuminati believe that they're at the top of the pyramid in the power structure. This is doubtful for the simple reason that the Jesuits' agenda is much more carefully hidden than that of the Illuminati. Many of us have been exposed to the term Illuminati through the mainstream media. By comparison, the operations of the Jesuit Order are known to very few. The higher up you go, the more secrecy you encounter.

The Jesuits use the Illuminati as a tool of misdirection. The media talk up the Illuminati in order to keep the Jesuit Order out of the spotlight. The same relationship exists between the Jesuits and the freemasons, who we'll cover in the next chapter.

1. "Illuminati." EncycloReader. Encyclopedia Britannica, 11th Edition, 1911. https://encycloreader.org/db/view.php?id=Gar3xGLUORCM

ΑΩ
THE FREEMASONS

Although the existence of freemasonry is far from secret, it is still referred to as a secret society. The term remains appropriate since the inner workings of the organization are opaque to outsiders. This opacity stems from the fact that masons are bound by an oath of secrecy. Regarding the origins of freemasonry, we have the following from Encyclopedia Britannica:

> The origins of freemasonry are not known definitively. National organized freemasonry began in 1717 with the founding of the Grand Lodge—an association of masonic lodges—in England. However, freemason societies have existed for much longer. The most popular theory is that freemasonry emerged out of the stonemasonry guilds of the Middle Ages.[1]

Freemasonry is a massive global organization. Harvard-educated historian Bernard Fay compiled a list of 170,000 members during WWII as part of an investigation into their criminal activities.[2] Freemasons appear to be divided into two major strata: a publicly visible level, open to all men over the age of 18, and a higher level about which very little is known. This hierarchical structure is evidenced by the fact that the publicly visible organization has only three commonly mentioned degrees, or levels: first degree (entered apprentice), second degree (fellowcraft), and third degree (master mason).[3]

Higher levels are infrequently mentioned on masons' websites, and go up to 33rd degree masons. This is a high honour awarded to master masons who have demonstrated exceptional fidelity to the masonic cause. Whenever we hear speculation about the influence of freemasonry on world events, the players are often identified as 33rd degree masons.[4]

There is speculation that the number 33 was chosen because it represents the age of Christ when He was crucified. Another theory is that it refers to the third of angels (33 per cent) who were banished from Heaven, as told in Revelation 12:4. These interpretations link freemasonry to the occult. However, the number 33 appears several times in the Bible without a negative connotation. For example, 1 Kings 2:11 tells us that King David ruled over Jerusalem for 33 years.[5]

Given that the number 33 frequently pops up in science, history, astrology, and many other areas of study, it can't be taken as conclusive evidence (on its own) that freemasonry is linked to Satanism. We need to dig deeper.

Freemasonry has been described as a cult because it has a religious belief system, including an all powerful deity who is referred to as the Grand Architect of the Universe. Masons come to the Lodge from all religions, but when they take their oath, this is the deity they worship. Nowhere in the masonic belief system is Jesus Christ acknowledged as the Saviour. Freemasons are not Christians.

There appear to be two distinct categories of masons, with a strong delineation between them. Lower level masons are linked to terms like fraternal well-being and brotherly love. However, the language changes when 33rd degree masons are discussed. In the place of brotherly love and charity, we see words like wisdom, knowledge and enlightenment. These high ranking members are the "pillars of leadership within the brotherhood."[6]

There's a popular hypothesis that the two categories of masons are essentially separate organizations. Lower level masons operate in total ignorance of 33rd degree masons' activities. Apprentices and fellows perform legitimate charitable works, and believe that their superiors do the same. They act as a cover for the clandestine pursuits of their superiors. It isn't until being promoted that their eyes are opened to the true agenda of freemasonry.

This is why the term secret society still fits. If anyone attempts to cast blame on freemasonry, the lower level masons can be held up as proof that the organization's goals are benign. Meanwhile, the 33rd degree masons continue to operate in the shadows with carte blanche to do as they wish.

For evidence that something is missing from the wholesome descriptions of freemasonry we see in the mainstream media, we need only examine some famous 33rd degree masons. The first one we'll look at is Aleister Crowley (1875-1947). This 33rd degree freemason is regarded as the most influential satanist of the 20th century. Crowley, a bisexual occultist, described himself as 'the beast' and practised black magic. Whether you believe he was an evil psychopath or just a deranged clown, the question to be asked is, why would a charitable organization that promotes brotherly love promote such an individual to their highest ranks?[7]

Another 33rd degree freemason was Giuseppe Mazzini (1805-1872), an Italian mercenary and revolutionary. Mazzini is linked to the birth of the mafia through his leadership role in La Giovine Italia (Young Italy). This was a revolutionary group that sought to overthrow the Italian government in the 19th century, and financed itself through robbery, extortion, and kidnapping. Mazzini is also known for his infamous correspondence with Albert Pike.[8]

General Albert Pike (1809-1891) was a 33rd degree freemason who was known as the pope of American masonry. According to some historians, he was instrumental in fomenting the insurrection of the South that led to the bloody U.S. Secession War (1860 -1865). For his heinous war crimes, Pike was sentenced by a military court and imprisoned.

In 1871, Pike corresponded with fellow mason Giuseppe Mazzini about establishing a plan to incite three world wars, with the end goal of leaving the world in such chaos that the freemasons would be able to create a one world government and offer a promise to restore international order under their command.[9]

"FOR THE MYSTERY OF INIQUITY DOTH ALREADY WORK" - 2 THESSALONIANS 2:7

Freemasons can often be found in political offices and include figures such as Sir Winston Churchill and several former U.S. presidents: George Washington, Theodore Roosevelt, Franklin D. Roosevelt, Harry Truman, and Gerald Ford.[10]

One of the best ways to learn about an organization is through former members who have documented their experiences. William Schnoebelen (1949-) was attracted to freemasonry because it appealed to his interest in the occult. A freemason for over ten years, he finally left the organization after finding out about the hidden corruption and satanic practices that are hidden from lower degree masons. He cowrote a book with his wife about his experiences as a mason, entitled *Lucifer Dethroned*.[11]

Another notable book is *The Lost Keys of Freemasonry* by 33rd degree Canadian mason Manly P. Hall (1901-1990). In the book, the author references 'Luciferian energy' and describes masonry as a type of religion.[12]

More recently, New Age guru and freemason David Spangler wrote a book called *Reflections on the Christ* in 1978. The most quoted line in the book is, "No one will enter the New World Order unless he or she will make a pledge to worship Lucifer. No one will enter the New Age unless they will take a Luciferian initiation."[13]

In summary, there's sufficient evidence to conclude that freemasonry is a dual level organization, with a lower level ostensibly dedicated to charitable works and a higher level hidden from the public eye. Higher level members are globalists with megalomaniacal ambitions. They consider freemasonry to be a unique religion that is supreme over all others. This religion is anti-Christian, and many, if not all high level masons are Satan worshippers.

Now that we've covered the history and operation of freemasonry, let's explore its connection to the Jesuit Order. The first clue that the two organizations are related is that freemason Albert Pike, mentioned earlier, was also a Jesuit: "Albert Pike (1809-1891) a Jesuit of Newbury Port moved to Arkansas where he became a prominent member of the secessionist movement."[14]

More evidence comes from historian James Parton (1822-1891), who said "If you trace up Masonry, through all its Orders, till you come to the grand tip-top head Mason of the World, you will discover that the dread individual and the Chief of the Society of Jesus [i.e., the Superior General of the Jesuit Order] are one and the same person."[15]

Parton does not say anything about the pecking order of the Jesuits and masons, but author David Nikao Wilcoxson provides strong evidence of Jesuit control over the freemasons in his web article "The Jesuit Order - The Society of Jesus."[16]

Given that the workings of the Jesuit Order are more opaque than freemasonry, Wilcoxson's conclusion seems sound. The masons are in the public eye for a reason. They're an instrument of misdirection—like the Illuminati—employed to keep everyone's eyes off the machinations of the Jesuit Order.

1. "What are the origins of Freemasonry?" Encyclopedia Britannica, https://www.britannica.com/question/What-are-the-origins-of-Freemasonry
2. Makow, Henry. "Historian Brought Freemasons to Heel" August 3, 2023, https://www.henrymakow.com/bernard_fay.html
3. "Degrees." Be A Freemason, https://beafreemason.org/degrees
4. Regal, William. "33rd Degree Mason: The Pinnacle Of Freemasonry." Freemasons Community, July 19, 2023. https://freemasonscommunity.life/33rd-degree-mason/
5. Grider, Geoffrey. "Master Number 33." Now the End Begins. March 20, 2020. https://www.nowtheendbegins.com/freemasonry-coronavirus-number-33-new-world-order/
6. Regal, William. "33rd Degree Mason: The Pinnacle Of Freemasonry." Freemasons Community, July 19, 2023. https://freemasonscommunity.life/33rd-degree-mason/
7. "Aleister Crowley: A Very Irregular Freemason." The Square Magazine. https://www.thesquaremagazine.com/mag/article/202208aleister-crowley-a-very-irregular-freemason/
8. Donahue, James. "MAFIA: The Modern-day Founder Guiseppi Mazzini Was A Rabid Globalist." The Millennium Report, January 21, 2019. https://themillenniumreport.com/2019/01/mafia-the-modern-day-founder-guiseppi-mazzini-was-a-rabid-globalist/
9. Duff, Gordon. "Freemasonry and Satanism: The History of Albert Pike." Veterans Today, August 24, 2019. https://

www.veteranstoday.com/2019/08/24/freemasonry-and-satanism-the-history-of-albert-pike/

10. "Famous Freemasons." Masons of California. https://freemason.org/famous-freemasons/

11. "Freemason Whistleblowers Expose the Secret World of Freemasonry." Dare To Fly. https://dare-to-fly.co.uk/freemason-whistleblowers-expose-the-secret-world-of-freemasonry/

12. Ibid.

13. Spangler, David. *Reflections on the Christ*. Words Distributing Co., California. 1978 pp. 44-45

14. "Category Archives: Albert Pike." JCEmmanuel. https://jcemmanuel.wordpress.com/category/albert-pike/

15. "The World is a Stage." January 31, 2022, Exposing the Darkness. https://lionessofjudah.substack.com/p/the-world-is-a-stage-klaus-schwab

16. Wilcoxson, David Nikao. "The Jesuit Order - The Society of Jesus." End Time Deceptions. https://christianitybeliefs.org/end-times-deceptions/the-jesuit-order-the-society-of-jesus/

AΩ
PROTESTANTISM UNDER ATTACK

The following chapters outline the multiple attacks that the Protestant Reformation has weathered since its inception half a millennium ago. We'll begin by exploring the Jesuit Treason, the corruption of Scripture, and the corruption of the Fourth Commandment. Then we'll study the infiltration of the Protestant Church by the Jesuit Order, focusing on case studies of the Anglican, Presbyterian and Seventh-day Adventist Churches.

We'll then look at the Jesuit infiltration of education, language and science. These centuries-long campaigns have had profoundly negative consequences for Protestantism as well as Christianity overall.

"PUT ON THE WHOLE ARMOUR OF GOD, THAT YE MAY BE ABLE TO STAND AGAINST THE WILES OF THE DEVIL."
- EPHESIANS 6:11

All these attacks have been spearheaded by the Jesuit Order, sometimes with the visible support of the papacy and sometimes surreptitiously. In several cases, the Jesuit Order's satellite organizations—the Illuminati and freemasons—have also been complicit.

ΑΩ
THE JESUIT TREASON

The Jesuit Treason, also known as the Gunpowder Plot, was a failed attempt at assassinating King James I of England in 1605. James I was a Protestant king who was seen by many as the political head of the Reform movement in Europe. This made him a Jesuit target of paramount importance.

The Jesuits knew that by assassinating James and replacing him with a Catholic monarch, they would gain a great victory against the Reformers. With a Catholic head of state, the Jesuits would be able to bring an entire nation back into the Catholic fold.

"WHOSO SHEDDETH MAN'S BLOOD, BY MAN SHALL HIS BLOOD BE SHED: FOR IN THE IMAGE OF GOD MADE HE MAN." - GENESIS 9:6

The plan was to blow up the House of Lords during the State Opening of England's Parliament. This would be followed by a popular revolt during which James's nine-year-old daughter, Princess Elizabeth, would be installed as the Catholic head of state.[1]

A Spanish mercenary by the name of Guy Fawkes was hired by Jesuit mastermind Henry Garnet (1555-1606) and his co-conspirators, Jesuits Oswald Tesmond and John

Gerard, to plant 36 barrels of gunpowder beneath the House of Parliament. Fawkes was discovered just moments before detonating the charges and was executed along with Garnet, Tesmond, Gerard, and several other parties involved in the plot.[2]

The failure of the assassination attempt against King James is commemorated every year on Guy Fawkes Night, when the English burn effigies of Fawkes to celebrate the foiling of the plot.

1. "10 Works, January 31 the anniversary of The Gunpowder Plot of 1605, or the Jesuit Treason." Zaidan Gallery. https://zaidan.blog/2023/01/31/10-works-january-31-the-anniversary-of-the-gunpowder-plot-of-1605-or-the-jesuit-treason/
2. "27 January 1606 – The trial of the Gunpowder Conspirators." The Tudor Society. https://www.tudorsociety.com/27-january-1606-trial-gunpowder-conspirators/

ΑΩ
THE CORRUPTION OF SCRIPTURE

Nearly eighty per cent of the world's bibles are distributed by United Bible Societies (UBS), an organization formed in 1946 that now includes 142 member societies, including those in the U.S., the U.K., and Canada.[1] In the years preceding the Second Vatican Council, a dialogue was begun between the UBS and the Roman Catholic Church (RCC) to facilitate cooperation in Bible translation between Catholics and Protestants.[2]

One of the dominant Catholic figures participating in this cooperative venture was Cardinal Augustine Bea (1881-1968), a Jesuit. After the death of Cardinal Bea in 1968, the UBS extended the invitation to join their editorial committee to another Jesuit, Carlo Maria Martini (1927-2012).[3]

"THEY PROFESS THAT THEY KNOW GOD, BUT IN WORKS THEY DENY HIM ..." - TITUS 1:16

The Bible translation chosen by the Jesuit controlled UBS project was the Greek New Testament (GNT) version, created by theologians Brooke Foss Westcott (1825-1901) and Fenton John Anthony Hort (1828-1892) in 1881. The GNT is an amalgam of various sources and is not based on the Textus Receptus (Latin for 'received text')—the New Testament manuscript upon which all the Protestant

Reformers based their translations. The GNT is the Bible version promoted by UBS, despite the fact that it is incompatible with the Textus Receptus.[4]

Westcott and Hort speculated, with no evidence to support their idea, that the authentic text of the New Testament had been lost for hundreds of years. They then went on to claim that it was not until the 19th century that the 'real' texts (which included the Codex Vaticanus) turned up. The Vaticanus text was conveniently 'rediscovered' in the Vatican library in 1845, where it had supposedly lain since 1481.[5]

If their claims were true, it means that Christians would have been without the Word of God for 1,500 years. This is hardly a defensible proposition, as God would not have permitted his Children to be without his guidance for so long.

To understand the scope of the disconnect, let's explore the differences between the Textus Receptus and the GNT. Textus Receptus is the New Testament in the original Greek, originating in Antioch, where Christians first gathered. It was used by the Reformers for the English and German translations that eventually evolved into the King James Version (KJV) Bible.

The KJV Bible is named after King James I of England (1566-1625), who commissioned a new English Bible translation in 1604. It superceded the Geneva Bible that was completed by Protestant scholars in 1560 and was later outlawed by King James. It was not the translation of the Geneva Bible that James objected to, but the annotations that it contained. Some annotations described monarchs as tyrants, calling into question the need to have a king as head of church and state.[6]

King James authorized the KJV Bible to be read in churches after it was first published in 1611. It became known as the Authorized Version in 1814—the standard among English speaking Christians.

The KJV Bible is considered the most accurate English translation in existence and the definitive version of Scripture. It built on the work of William Tyndale and Myles Cloverdale, who created the first complete English Bible by adding the books of the Old Testament that Tyndale had not included. A skilled committee of 54 scholars worked for seven years to complete the KJV Bible.[7]

The KJV Bible is the cornerstone of Protestantism. It is the most painstakingly produced Bible ever created, and widely regarded as the inerrant Word of God. It is also the longest lived and most widely read Bible in history. In contrast, the GNT is a compilation of various manuscripts and fragments. It incorporates the Codex Vaticanus, the Codex Alexandrinus, the Codex Sinaiticus, and also takes into account ancient copies of the New Testament in Latin (including the Latin Vulgate) and ancient Syriac.[8]

The common flaw of early Catholic Church Bibles was the fact that they were written in Latin. These Latin Bibles had been poorly translated from the original Greek and were corrupted. To get a sense of how inaccurate these versions were, let's look at Codex Vaticanus as an example. The Vaticanus gospel alone, when compared to the Textus Receptus, omits 2,877 words, adds 536, substitutes 935, transposes 2,098, and modifies 1,132. It should be noted that these discrepancies are not minor in nature, but result in substantial changes in the meaning of the text.[9]

The English Standard Version (ESV) Bible, the New International Version (NIV) and other modern Bibles are based on the GNT, and are missing many words that validate the deity of Jesus Christ.[10] This is not surprising when considering the assertion made by some historians that Westcott and Hort were Jesuit agents.[11]

The latest sales figures for English Bible translations in the U.S. show that the popularity of the KJV Bible is gradually declining. It dropped from second to fifth place over an 18-month period. At the end of 2022, the top ranked Bible translations in the U.S. (in descending order by sales) were:

1. New International Version (NIV)
2. English Standard Version (ESV)
3. New Living Translation (NLT)
4. Christian Standard Bible (CSB)
5. King James Version (KJV)
6. New King James Version (NKJV)
7. Reina Valera (RV)
8. New International Reader's Version (NIrV)
9. New Revised Standard Version (NRSV)
10. New American Standard Bible (NASB)[12]

There seems to be a concerted effort on the part of Bible publishers to promote corrupt Bible translations like the NIV and ESV. The KJV Bible naturally requires more effort to read. However, if the drop in popularity of the KJV Bible was simply due to our ever decreasing attention spans, the decline would have been much more gradual.

The Bible was never intended to be an easy read. For the English speaker, the most complete understanding of Scripture will come from using the most accurate translation: the KJV Bible. Reading the KJV Bible requires more work, but also rewards the reader with a fuller and more precise understanding of the Word of God.

Many theologians describe the KJV Bible as a work of art—not in the sense that it contains poetic passages—but in recognition of the intricacy of its design. There is an entirely separate layer of understanding that can be gleaned from Scripture by identifying and interpreting the many patterns that have been woven into it. These patterns are based on occurrences of specific numbers and their association with certain words and phrases. The patterns are most prevalent in the English KJV Bible and are frequently not found at all in other versions.

Let's look at some examples. The number '7' signifies completeness and perfection. It is the number most closely associated with God. This number can be seen throughout the Bible, from the beginning verses of Genesis that describe the seven days of Creation, to the concluding verses of Revelation. What many readers don't realize is that the number describes the frequency of usage of certain words and phrases. For example, in the English KJV Bible, there are exactly seven mentions of the following words and phrases:

- ► The Word
- ► My Beloved Son
- ► His Son
- ► Firstborn
- ► Holy Spirit
- ► Thunders (God's voice)[13]

This is just one example of the hundreds of patterns that can be found. One particularly significant observation that theologians have made is that the 1611th mention of the word 'Lord' in the Bible is found in Deuteronomy 16:11—and it gets even more interesting. This verse reads:

And thou shalt rejoice before the Lord thy God, thou, and thy son, and thy daughter, and thy manservant, and thy maidservant, and the Levite that is within thy gates, and the stranger, and the fatherless, and the widow, that are among you, in the place which the Lord thy God hath chosen to place his name there.

Note the last phrase, referencing the place where God has chosen to place His name. This is the 49th mention of the phrase 'His name' in the Bible. As we saw earlier in the chapter, 7 is God's number, and 7 times 7 equals 49.[14]

What makes all this significant is that the King James Bible was published in the year 1611. Connecting the dots, we have clear evidence that the English KJV Bible is the version of Scripture chosen by God.[15]

The significance of the number '7' is demonstrated not only within the pages of the King James Bible, but applies to the Bible itself. The KJV Bible was the seventh English language translation of the Bible produced that was based on the original Hebrew and Greek texts.[16] Each successive translation improved upon the preceding version, culminating in the KJV Bible. This iterative process, which spanned many decades, is actually referenced in Psalms 12:6-7:

The words of the Lord are pure words: as silver tried in a furnace of earth, purified seven times.

Thou shalt keep them, O Lord, thou shalt preserve them from this generation for ever.

The evidence showing that the KJV Bible is the inerrant Word of God is overwhelming. It is no coincidence that it is the Bible that has been read by the greatest number of people worldwide.

1. "The United Bible Societies and Rome." Way of Life Literature. https://www.wayoflife.org/database/biblesocieties.html
2. "Bible - Versions and Translations." Teaching the Word Ministries. http://www.teachingtheword.org/apps/articles/? view=post&columnid=5450&articleid=199400
3. Ibid.
4. Ibid.
5. "Why Use The King James Bible?" King James Bible Research Council. https://kjbrc.org/why-use-the-king-james-bible/
6. "The Geneva Bible Banned by King James in Late Medieval England." Brewminate. https://brewminate.com/the-geneva-bible-banned-by-king-james-in-late-medieval-england/
7. "King James Version." King James Bible Online. https:// www.kingjamesbibleonline.org/King-James-Version/
8. "Bible - Versions and Translations." Teaching the Word Ministries. http://www.teachingtheword.org/apps/articles/? view=post&columnid=5450&articleid=199400
9. "The Preserved Bible." https://www.youtube.com/watch? v=Pw6Anlxupd4
10. Wilcoxson, David Nikao. "The Two Paths of New Testament Manuscripts." End Time Deceptions. https://christianitybeliefs.org/ end-times-deceptions/bible-manuscript-paths/
11. "Secret Societies' Attack Upon the Holy Bible 6: Dean Burgon's Testimony." The Overlords of Chaos. https:// www.overlordsofchaos.com/index.php?view=category&id=125
12. Rainer, Thom. "Bestselling Bible Translations at the End of 2022." Church Answers. https://churchanswers.com/blog/bestselling-bible-translations-at-the-end-of-2022/
13. "The King James Code." https://www.biblebelievers.com/ Hoggard_KJV_Code.html
14. "The 1611th Mention of LORD (And Why It's a Really Big Deal)." Truth Is Christ. https://www.youtube.com/watch?v=yS78mFJcvhQ
15. "The Significance of the 1611th LORD Mention." Eightify. https:// eightify.app/summary/productivity-and-creativity/the-significance-of-the-1611th-lord-mention
16. "PROOF The King James Bible Is The Pure Word Of God / Hugo Talks #KJB." Hugo Talks. https://hugotalks.substack.com/p/proof-the-king-james-bible-is-the

AΩ

THE CORRUPTION OF THE FOURTH COMMANDMENT

The Fourth Commandment states:

Remember the Sabbath Day, to keep it holy. Six days shalt thou labor, and do all thy work: But the seventh day is the Sabbath of the Lord thy God.

There is general agreement among Biblical scholars that the Sabbath falls on Saturday, the last day of the week. This should be obvious to speakers of many languages in which the word for Saturday derives from the word 'Sabbath.' Thus we have 'sabado' in Spanish and 'sabato' in Italian, for example.

"AND GOD BLESSED THE SEVENTH DAY, AND SANCTIFIED IT: BECAUSE THAT IN IT HE HAD RESTED FROM ALL HIS WORK WHICH GOD CREATED AND MADE." - GENESIS 2:3

One would think that nothing could be easier than to respect a Commandment as simple and straightforward as this. It's no more difficult for us to rest on the day commanded by God than any other day. However, following this Commandment has proven to be more difficult than anyone could have possibly imagined. It's ironic that the one commandment that begins with the word 'remember' is the one Christians are most likely to forget. The assumption is that because the vast majority of churches conduct services on Sunday, that this must be the correct day on which to rest. This is a classic example of the danger of putting blind trust in authority. If your church teaches you to rest on Sunday, then it is leading you astray. As we'll see in this chapter, the blame for corrupting the Fourth Commandment falls on multiple parties.

The failure of most Christians to obey the Fourth Commandment is a consequence of events that predate both the Catholic and Protestant churches. Ignatius of Antioch, who lived in Syria from 35 to 108 AD, advocated a Sunday Sabbath in his Letter to Magnesians:

> Let us therefore no longer keep the Sabbath after the Jewish manner, and rejoice in days of idleness; for "he that does not work, let him not eat." For say the [holy] oracles, "In the sweat of thy face shalt thou eat thy bread." But let every one of you keep the Sabbath after a spiritual manner, rejoicing in meditation on the law, not in relaxation of the body, admiring the workmanship of God, and not eating things prepared the day before, nor using lukewarm drinks, and walking within a prescribed space, nor finding delight in dancing and plaudits which have no sense in them. And after the observance of the Sabbath, let every friend of Christ keep the Lord's Day as a festival, the resurrection-day, the queen and chief of all the days [of the week].[1]

The Roman emperor Constantine converted to Christianity in 312 AD, beginning a slow process that would eventually see Rome adopting Christianity as its state religion in 380 AD. Constantine recognized the importance of making this transition palatable to the masses. He did this by carrying the Pagan tradition of Sunday worship into Christianity. Sunday worship became entrenched as a pillar of Roman Catholicism.

Solid evidence of the original Catholic position on the Sabbath can be found in The Catechism of the Council of Trent, published in 1566. It tells us the following:

The Sabbath, Why Changed To Sunday
But the Church of God has thought it well to transfer the celebration and observance of the Sabbath to Sunday. For, as on that day light first shone on the world, so by the Resurrection of our Redeemer on the same day, by whom was thrown open to us the gate to eternal life, we were called out of darkness into light; and hence the Apostles would have it called the Lord's day. We also learn from the Sacred Scriptures that the first day of the week was held sacred because on that day the work of creation commenced, and on that day the Holy Ghost was given to the Apostles.[2]

Curiously, the Catholic position appears to have changed over time. It is still defiant, but now manages to defy the Catechism as well. At www.catholic.com we find the following:

Question:
Until recently, I always thought Catholics worshiped on the Sabbath, and that the early Church moved the Sabbath from Saturday to Sunday. Is this true?

Answer:
This is a common misunderstanding. Catholics do not worship on the Sabbath, which according to Jewish law is the last day of the week (Saturday), when God rested from all the work he had done in Creation (Gen. 2:2-3). Catholics worship on the Lord's Day, the first day of the

week (Sunday, the eighth day); the day when God said "Let there be light" (Gen. 1:3); the day when Christ rose from the dead; the day when the Holy Spirit came upon the Apostles (Day of Pentecost). The Catechism of the Catholic Church says: "The Church celebrates the day of Christ's Resurrection on the 'eighth day,' Sunday, which is rightly called the Lord's Day" (CCC 2191).[3]

As we'll see later in this chapter, the Lord's Day is not Sunday, but refers to the day of the Second Coming of Jesus Christ. The argument provided by www.catholic.com is invalid because it rests on a false assumption.

Martin Luther felt that a clean break from Jewish tradition was needed, so he advocated observance of the Sabbath on Sunday rather than Saturday. By the same token, he was against the Jewish tradition of circumcision and felt that Protestants should not partake in it.

Daniel Walther, Professor of Church History (Seventh-day Adventist), writes:

> While Luther repeatedly asserted that the commandments were not repealed by Christ, yet he thought that there was no need of observing the seventh-day Sabbath. He considered the Sabbath as pertaining to the Mosaic ceremonial law. When somebody asked him, "But did not Jesus Himself say that not a jot or a tittle of the law shall pass away?" Luther retorted: Jesus was not speaking of the ceremonial law but of the moral law, which was in existence long before Moses and the patriarchs. It is, in fact, the universal law of humanity, though Moses gave the clearest expression to it. Similarly, the Sabbath or rest day is a universal law in order that the people may assemble for the worship of God. But that they should assemble on the seventh day applies only in the case of

69

the Jews, and the observance of this day is not incumbent on other peoples.

He argued repeatedly that those who kept the Jewish Sabbath should also practice circumcision. He said, "If Carlstadt writes more about the Sabbath, Sunday must give way and the Sabbath—that is, Saturday—must be kept holy. He would really in all things make Jews out of us and require circumcision."[4]

To critique Luther's response, placing equal weight on Sabbath keeping and circumcision is hardly defensible in light of the fact that the former is a Commandment and the latter is not. Moreover, the notion that following the Sabbath would make a Jew out of someone is misplaced. Whether or not Christians and Jews rest on the same day is irrelevant. The core of Luther's philosophy was Sola Scriptura—Scripture above all else. Since the Bible makes it very clear that the Sabbath is to be observed on Saturday—and enshrines it as the Fourth Commandment—it is clear that in this instance, Luther did not honour his own standard.

There is a commonly held belief among Protestants that Sunday is the Lord's Day (the day Christ was resurrected), and this supposedly makes Sunday observance of the Sabbath acceptable. The Book of Revelation (1:10) speaks of the Lord's Day, but there is no Scriptural evidence that it refers to Sunday (or any day of the week for that matter). A more believable interpretation is that the Lord's Day in Revelation refers to the day of the Second Coming of Christ. Rev. Matthew Bryce Ervin asserts:

The "Lord's day" is to be more literally translated as a "lordian day." This is what is referred to elsewhere in the Bible as the "Day of the LORD." Honestly, this understanding should be readily evident to anyone reading through his Bible and coming across common terms. The "Day of the LORD" is used nineteen times in the Old Testament and four times in the New Testament. In addition to this it is called "that day" quite often. This phrase is used to describe historical events that have already occurred (as types pointing to the final "Day"). But it ultimately refers to a time of great trouble (Joel 2:30-32, Zech. 14:1, Mal. 4:1,5, etc.) and the visitation of the Lord upon the earth (Zech. 14:4, 1 Pet. 2:12, etc.). The sublime purpose of the Lord's day is told to us by the prophet Isaiah.

The pride of man will be humbled And the loftiness of men will be abased; And the LORD alone will be exalted in that day. Isaiah 2:17

John's apocalypse is covering the Day of the LORD as the book is recording what the Tribulation will entail and the Second Coming of Christ. So the "Lord's day" in Revelation 1:10 is easily understood in the context of John writing to seven Churches to inform them that he was shown a vision of the "Day of the LORD."[5]

Based on the available evidence, we can conclude that both Luther and the Catholic Church erred in failing to entrench the Sabbath on Saturday (albeit for entirely different reasons). Rather than dealing with the issue in an honest and forthright manner, Protestant church leaders have concocted a bewildering array of excuses for not observing the Fourth Commandment. One of the most egregious of these is the suggestion that the coming of Christ obviated the Old Covenant (the Ten Commandments). Although we were blessed with a New Covenant, nowhere in the Bible does it say that this New Covenant absolves us of the need to obey the Ten Commandments. Christ states in Matthew 5:17:

Think not that I am come to destroy the law, or the prophets: I am not come to destroy, but to fulfil.

No significant developments took place regarding the observance of the Sabbath until the 19th century. New Protestant denominations emerged which entrenched the Sabbath as the day of rest in their doctrine. These include the Seventh-day Adventist (SDA) Church, the Seventh-day Baptist Church, the Church of God, the United Sabbath Day Church, and others. However, there doesn't appear to be any instance of an older Protestant denomination recognizing its error and moving its observed day of rest from Sunday to Saturday. This is a missed opportunity.

The Fourth Commandment is a very special one because its roots go all the way back to the Book of Genesis. God created the earth in six days and rested on the seventh. When we observe the Sabbath, we are commemorating the seventh day of Creation and following in our Creator's footsteps.

1. "Ignatius to the Magnesians." Early Christian Writings. https://www.earlychristianwritings.com/text/ignatius-magnesians-longer.html
2. *The Catechism of the Council of Trent.* 1566 (English translation 1923.), p. 243.
3. "Did the Early Church Move the Sabbath from Saturday to Sunday?" https://www.catholic.com/qa/did-the-early-church-move-the-sabbath-from-saturday-to-sunday
4. Walther, Daniel. "Is There a Relationship Between Luther and Seventh-day Adventists?" The Ministry for World Evangelism, July 1955, Number 7, p. 39. https://www.ministrymagazine.org/archive/1955/07/is-there-a-relationship-between-luther-and-seventh-day-adventists
5. "The 'Lord's Day' in Revelation 1:10 is Not Sunday." June 7, 2013. https://appleeye.org/2013/06/07/the-lords-day-in-revelation-110-is-not-sunday/

ΑΩ

THE INFILTRATION OF THE PROTESTANT MOVEMENT

Campaigns were orchestrated by the Jesuit Order to infiltrate not only the Protestant Church, but also the education system, the English language (particularly with respect to certain words that pertain to Protestantism), and several fields of science. These campaigns were carried out by installing Jesuits, Illuminati and freemasons in key government and industry positions, and leveraging their influence to bend educational, linguistic and scientific developments to the will of the Jesuit Order. This took place in Europe and later in the New World as well. Let's begin by looking at the infiltration of the Protestant Church.

Much in the same way that the CIA infiltrated the U.S. media, the Jesuits quietly installed agents in Protestant churches all over the world to undermine the teachings of Martin Luther and attempt to bring Protestant doctrine back in line with that of the Roman Catholic Church (RCC). The process has been slow and gradual, done over the course of many decades so as to escape notice. Author Shaun Willcock writes:

Just a few short years after the founding of the Order, the Jesuits had established seminaries on the continent of Europe for the purpose of training young English noblemen as Roman Catholic missionaries. These men, when their training was complete, were sent back to Britain as traitors, to once again subjugate the land to the pope of Rome. In 1551, the Council of Trent sent secret instructions to the Jesuits of Paris on how to undermine and destroy the "Church of England". A copy, accidentally dropped by a Jesuit priest in a pulpit in 1568, was found. The instructions were these: Ye are not to preach all after one method but observe the place wherein you come.

If Lutheranism be prevalent, then preach Calvinism; if Calvinism, then Lutheranism; if in England, then either of them, or John Huss' opinions, Anabaptism, or any that are contrary to the Holy See of St. Peter, by which your function will not be suspected, and yet you may still act on the interest of Mother Church; there being, as the Council are agreed on, no better way to demolish that Church (the Church of England) of heresy, but by mixture of doctrines, and by adding of ceremonies more than at present permitted. Some of you who undertook to be of this sort of Heretical Episcopal Society, bring it as near to the Mother Church as you can; for then the Lutheran party, the Calvinists, the Anabaptists and other heretics, will be averse thereto, and thereby make the Episcopal heresy odious to all these, and be a means to reduce all in time to Mother Church.[1]

   The classic divide and conquer strategy outlined in this quote was employed by Jesuit spies to considerable effect. For specific examples of Jesuit infiltration of the Protestant Church, plentiful evidence can be found. The Southern Evangelical Seminary of North Carolina in the United States was founded in 1992 by Norman Geisler (1932-2019), who holds a Ph.D. in philosophy from Jesuit Loyola University. He also became a member of the American Philosophical Society in 1968, an organization that includes members with an interest in the occult. His book, *Roman Catholics and Evangelicals: Agreements and Differences*, is an effort to unite Protestants and Catholics. This is evidenced in the book's conclusion:

> In this final section we wish to end on a positive note, firmly believing that a cooperative effort between Roman Catholics and evangelicals could be the greatest social force for good in America. ... Our common doctrinal and moral beliefs are too large, and the need in America for a united voice on them is too great for us to dwell on our differences to the neglect of crucial cooperation needed to fight the forces of evil in our society and our world.[2]

Geisler's colleague Ross Rhoads (1932-2017), a pastor of Calvary Church (also in North Carolina) was a member of the Council of 56, an organization with ties to the CIA, the Council on Foreign Relations, the Trilateral Group, and freemasons. Rhoads also had ties to Billy Graham.[3]

The term televangelist is synonymous with Billy Graham (1918-2018), one of the most well known religious personalities of the 20th century. He was a southern Baptist minister who rode to fame under the wing of media mogul William Randolph Hearst (1863-1951).

During the 1950s, U.S. president Dwight D. Eisenhower (1890-1969) promoted the phrase Judeo-Christian—an oxymoron—to dupe Americans into believing that two antithetical value systems could be combined into one. The goal was to unite Protestants and Jews in support of American imperialist ambitions. Hearst was a personal friend of Eisenhower, and saw Billy Graham as the ideal agent to promote Eisenhower's catchphrase. Who could have guessed that by simply linking them with a hyphen, Jewish and Christian values could magically be made to align?

Discussing Judeo-Christian values makes about as much sense as discussing Sino-Senegalese or Homo-Heterosexual values. Nevertheless, this hyphenated linguistic gremlin has managed to burrow into the collective Western psyche and stay there. To this day, politicians trumpet the phrase with gusto at every opportunity while doing their best to keep a straight face.

Billy Graham thus began his rise to fame as a star promoter of pro-Eisenhower propaganda under the Evangelical moniker. He did more than any other religious figure in U.S. history to promote Zionism to American Christians.[4]

At the peak of his career, Graham had one of the largest worldwide audiences of any modern day minister. Beginning in 1989, a series of satellite broadcasts extended his preaching to audiences in more than 185 countries and territories.[5]

Graham may have started his career in the ministry with sincere intentions. However, he became indebted to Hearst for catapulting him to fame, and was subsequently unable to do anything without his approval.[6] He was no doubt fully aware that he was being used to promote an agenda not of his own making, yet continued on this path until he had completely betrayed his Christian roots.

Graham was a 33rd degree freemason. He had a Jesuit handler, a Catholic bishop by the name of Fulton Sheen (1895-1979). Sheen was often euphemistically referred to as his mentor. He was a televangelist as well, and was noted for his attempts at reconciling Protestant and Catholic doctrine. This became yet another agenda that Graham was coerced into promoting. In his 1997 autobiography, Graham elaborated his ecumenical beliefs

76

and championed close cooperation between Protestantism and Catholicism.[7]

"AND THAT BECAUSE OF FALSE BRETHREN UNAWARES BROUGHT IN, WHO CAME IN PRIVILY TO SPY OUT OUR LIBERTY WHICH WE HAVE IN CHRIST JESUS, THAT THEY MIGHT BRING US INTO BONDAGE" - GALATIANS 2:4

The fact that all the aforementioned figures are linked demonstrates that the push towards ecumenism is being driven by a central force. Geisler, Rhoads, Graham and Sheen all served the same agenda and all had ties to the Jesuits.

It's difficult to estimate how many more Protestant ministers are tangled in this web. If some of the most influential figures in the Protestant Church, like Billy Graham, have been pushing ecumenism at the behest of their Jesuit handlers, it stands to reason that ministers in virtually every denomination are under pressure to do the same.

1. Willcock, Shaun. "A Brief History of the Jesuits." The Other Side. https://thebibleistheotherside.org/newsitem25.htm
2. "Jesuit Infiltration of the Evangelical Church." Fanatic for Jesus, January 25, 2012. https://fanaticforjesus.blogspot.com/2012/01/jesuit-infiltration-of-evangelical.html
3. Ibid.
4. "America's Church: The Invention of the Evangelical Christian Movement." Striker, Eric. The Unz Review, January 24, 2024. https://www.unz.com/estriker/americas-church-the-invention-of-the-evangelical-christian-movement/#comments
5. "Billy Graham 1918-2018 Biography." Billy Graham 1918-2018. https://memorial.billygraham.org/biography/

6. "The Untold Story of Billy Graham." Jim Duke Perspective, February 26, 2018. https://jimdukeperspective.com/story-behind-billy-graham/
7. Ibid.

$A\Omega$

THE INFILTRATION OF THE ANGLICAN CHURCH

The Jesuit Order did not abandon its quest to bring England back into the Catholic fold after its failed assassination attempt on King James I. The Jesuits implemented a new strategy, installing spies and Catholic priests in Oxford University and the Church of England in an attempt to subvert the church from within. This campaign came to be known as the Oxford Movement. It began in 1833.

The leader of the Oxford Movement was John Henry Newman (1801-1890), an academic at Oxford who was ordained in the Anglican Church and later became a cardinal in the Catholic Church. Leveraging their influence at Oxford University, Newman and his Jesuit collaborators used textual criticism of the KJV Bible to turn members of the clergy back to the Catholic Church. Between 1833 and 1841, they published a series of leaflets called "Tracts for the Times." These papers were advertised as being against the papacy. However, without exception, the leaflets claimed that the KJV Bible was flawed and that Britons needed to return to the Catholic Church.

By undermining the KJV Bible, the Jesuits were essentially undermining the Anglican Church. This tactic proved very successful in sowing doubt in the Anglican clergy. In 1830, the number of priests in England was 434, and 16 of these had converted to Catholicism; in 1863 they numbered 1,242, and 162 had converted.[1]

"THAT WE HENCEFORTH BE NO MORE CHILDREN, TOSSED TO AND FRO, AND CARRIED ABOUT WITH EVERY WIND OF DOCTRINE, BY THE SLEIGHT OF MEN, AND CUNNING CRAFTINESS, WHEREBY THEY LIE IN WAIT TO DECEIVE;" - EPHESIANS 4:14

In his 1899 book *The Secret History of the Oxford Movement*, Walter Walsh asserted that many of the key players in the movement, including Newman, Pusey, and Keble, were not converts, but Jesuit assets from the beginning. Walsh also noted that it was during the Oxford Movement that the Oxford University Press, a subsidiary of the university, began to publish and promote the Scofield Reference Bible.[2] This heavily annotated Bible put a dispensationalist spin on Scripture to counter the Reformist argument that the papacy was the antichrist.

The Anglican Church never recovered from the Jesuit infiltration that began two centuries ago. Prior to the Oxford Movement, the vast majority of Britons considered themselves members of the church. Statistics show that Catholics now account for the largest portion of Christians in the UK, at 25 per cent, whereas the figure for Anglicans has plummeted to 21 per cent.[3]

1. "Wescott And Hort — The Overthrow of the Greek Text." Coercion Code: "Dark Times Are Upon Us." https://coercioncode.com/2021/05/18/wescott-and-hort-the-overthrow-of-the-greek-text/
2. "THE SECRET HISTORY OF THE OXFORD MOVEMENT by Walter Walsh." James Flory's Memory-Holed Book Reviews. https://

jamesflory.wordpress.com/2014/06/06/the-secret-history-of-the-oxford-movement-by-walter-walsh/

3. "Christianity in the UK." Faith Survey. https://faithsurvey.co.uk/uk-christianity.html

ΑΩ
THE INFILTRATION OF THE PRESBYTERIAN CHURCH

The Presbyterian Church in the U.S. has a national committee with the authority to make sweeping changes in how worship services are conducted in the church. The committee has enacted many changes over the years, including the following:

- To combat sexism, the hymns "God Rest Ye Merry, Gentlemen," "Faith of Our Fathers," and "Once to Every Man and Nation" were dropped
- To combat violence, the hymns "Onward, Christian Soldiers" and "The Battle Hymn of the Republic" were dropped
- To combat discrimination against the handicapped, the hymn "Stand, Up, Stand Up for Jesus!" was dropped

These changes were made without consulting the 2.9 million person membership of the church to see what their opinion might be.[1]

In 2013, the hymn "In Christ Alone" was dropped due to a heated debate about a line in the song that didn't seem appropriate to some committee members. The writers of the song refused to change a line referring to God that some members objected to.[2]

It's difficult to make sense of the rampant micromanaging in the service of political correctness that is going on in the Presbyterian church. Banning hymns over petty details points to a bureaucratic mindset that borders on hysteria.

"I HAVE GONE ASTRAY LIKE A LOST SHEEP" - PSALM 119:176

Freemasons have a long-standing connection with the Presbyterian Church. In 1889, 59 Presbyterian ministers were freemasons. Examples of Presbyterian masons who have held positions on the functional church level include names such as Robert W. Cretney (33rd degree, deacon Presbyterian church), Morton P. Steyer (KT, 32nd degree, Shriner, York Rite College, Royal Order of Scotland, and elder Presbyterian Church), and Hugh I. Evans (33rd degree, KT, National Head of the Presbyterian Church, USA).

33rd degree mason Hugh I. Evans (1887-1958), who represented the U.S. at the meeting of the World Council of Churches in Holland in 1948, was the National Head of the Presbyterian Church, U.S.A. in 1950-51. In 1955, he became the director of the Foundation of the Presbyterian Church at NYC and served for a while as the President of the Board of National Missions.[3]

Here's a telling anecdote about a Presbyterian churchgoer who observed the influence of masonry in his church first-hand:

I grew up going to a little neighbourhood Presbyterian church during the 1960's. The pastor and his wife and two girls lived on my street, within view of my driveway.

They were very nice people. The reverend sincerely lived according to his sermons. He wasn't a Freemason and wouldn't have been interested in such prideful, dark clubs.

But most of the fathers living around him and on my street were Masons. Shiners, in fact. They all joined my pastor's church and enrolled their sons there. The became his volunteer deacons, and were the main contributors to his church.

One Sunday when I was about 14, I noticed something I'd overlooked before. The Masons took up the front row of the seats, looking very intimidating in the black suits and black ties. Their faces looked cold and hard in contrast to the pastor who was soft.

Through intuition, I realized the Masons controlled the pastor. They had him by the balls. Shortly after, the synod transferred the pastor to start a new church in a new neighbourhood in another town. The new pastor struck me as a phoney snake and I wouldn't be surprised if he was a Mason, because he and they immediately got along.

The new pastor preached the new "improved" Gospel. Something was missing. So I started smoking and quit going to church in 1969. That is exactly how it works. It's simple. They just become a church's biggest funder and that's all it takes.[4]

The misfortunes of the Presbyterian Church started many decades ago with the freemasons, and the random hysterics of today's weak-minded church leaders are hastening its decline. When political correctness takes precedence over Scripture, the results are guaranteed to be nothing less than catastrophic.

1. "Subversion: Death From Within." EWTN. https://www.ewtn.com/catholicism/library/subversion-death-from-within-9547
2. Smietana, Bob. "Presbyterians stir debate by rejecting popular new hymn." Presbyterian Church USA, August 8, 2013. https://www.pcusa.org/news/2013/8/8/presbyterians-stir-debate-rejecting-popular-new-hy/
3. "Masons Have Played Prominent Roles In The Presbyterian Church." Wilmington for Christ, May 20, 2023. https://www.wilmingtonfavs.com/world-order/masons-have-played-prominent-roles-in-the-presbyterian-church.html
4. "Freemasons control most Protestant sects." Reader comment. https://www.henrymakow.com/2017/03/freemasons-control-most-protestant-sects.html

ΑΩ
THE INFILTRATION OF THE SDA CHURCH

American author and Seventh-day Adventist (SDA) theologian Danny Vierra (1953-2017) produced an excellent video in 2014 that can be seen on YouTube, called "Jesuits in the SDA Church." Part 1 of the video outlines how the SDA struggled to fend off attacks on doctrine from Jesuit agents Leroy Edwin Froom and Roy Allen Anderson in the 1950s.[1]

In Part 2 of the video, Vierra laments the watering down of SDA doctrine by ecumenism and spiritualism over the last several decades at the hands of the Roman Catholic Church (RCC). He also laments the reluctance of SDA principals to name the papacy as the antichrist, and discusses his work in exposing theologian and SDA member Samuele Bacchiocchi (1939-2008) as a Jesuit agent who campaigned to weaken the Adventist belief that the papacy is the antichrist.[2]

Part 3 of the video covers the negative influence of former North American SDA President Neal Wilson, who in 1976 echoed Bacchiocchi in denying that the papacy is the antichrist. The video also outlines various meetings and conferences held between the SDA and the RCC that were designed to promote unity of doctrine between the two churches.[3]

As a leading champion of SDA doctrine, Vierra fought to keep Adventists true to SDA principles. He was accused of

Catholic bashing and was repeatedly harassed by RCC officials who used their influence to orchestrate his excommunication from the SDA Church. To smooth things over with the RCC, SDA officials offered up Vierra as a sacrificial lamb and ousted him from the church.

"IF ANY MAN TEACH OTHERWISE, AND CONSENT NOT TO WHOLESOME WORDS, EVEN THE WORDS OF OUR LORD JESUS CHRIST . . . FROM SUCH WITHDRAW THYSELF." - 1 TIMOTHY 6:3-5

The SDA Church hasn't been fully compromised; there are still members who uphold its doctrine and aren't afraid to express their views. One such person is vlogger Greg Sereda, who runs a YouTube channel called Bible Flock Box. Sereda has a strong knowledge of Scripture and a knack for taking complex biblical concepts and putting them into simple language.

The types of events that have taken place in the Anglican, Presbyterian and SDA Churches are by no means exclusive to these churches. All major Protestant denominations have weathered similar setbacks. The whole of organized Protestantism has been irrevocably weakened by Jesuit infiltration.

1. "Jesuits in the Seventh Day Adventist Church!" Modern Manna Ministries. https://www.youtube.com/watch?v=CxvOgl8ht0M&list=PLLRhCOK0qiFCRXHLfOsoc2WQYH77_mO-e
2. "Jesuits in the SDA Church - Part 2." Modern Manna Ministries. https://www.youtube.com/watch?v=cb5mCMEFtlg
3. "Jesuits in the SDA Church - Part 3." Modern Manna Ministries. https://www.youtube.com/watch?v=5qbFBOHo7-w

ΑΩ
THE INFILTRATION OF EDUCATION

As the shock troops of the Counter-Reformation, the Jesuits did everything in their power to quell Protestant ideology. One such tactic was establishing control over education. They undertook the construction of numerous Jesuit colleges throughout Europe. These colleges were expressly designed to promote the Catholic Church as the 'one true church' and discredit Protestantism.

The first Jesuit college opened in Messina, Italy in 1548. By 1615 there were 372 colleges, and by 1755, the number had risen to 728.[1] Today, the global Jesuit education network represents over 2,700 Institutions and education projects employing over 200,000 faculty and staff in over 90 countries.[2] The Association of Jesuit Colleges and Universities in the U.S. states that "A Jesuit education is grounded in the liberal arts tradition with a focus on quality teaching, critical thinking, and rigorous academic standards and scholarship."[3]

The Jesuits have always been well aware of the malleability of young minds and the opportunities that can be gained by controlling the education system. They leveraged their stewardship of Catholic education to the fullest extent, incorporating anti-Reformation philosophy into the curricula of Jesuit schools. The following quote from ex-Jesuit and Illuminati principle Adam Weishaupt is an excellent summary of how the Jesuits conducted their strategy in Bavaria:

The degree of power to which the representatives of the Society of Jesus had been able to attain in Bavaria was all but absolute. Members of the order were the confessors and preceptors of the electors; hence they had a direct influence upon the policies of government. The censorship of religion had fallen into their eager hands, to the extent that some of the parishes even were compelled to recognize their authority and power. To exterminate all Protestant influence and to render the Catholic establishment complete, they had taken possession of the instruments of public education. It was by Jesuits that the majority of the Bavarian colleges were founded, and by them they were controlled. By them also the secondary schools of the country were conducted.[4]

Today, post-secondary Jesuit teaching stresses critical thinking and has a strong ecumenical component. It doesn't exhibit any strict adherence to Scripture, and students attending Jesuit colleges often describe the environment as informal and not overtly Catholic.

"BEWARE LEST ANY MAN SPOIL YOU THROUGH PHILOSOPHY AND VAIN DECEIT, AFTER THE TRADITION OF MEN, AFTER THE RUDIMENTS OF THE WORLD, AND NOT AFTER CHRIST" - COLOSSIANS 2:8

The Jesuit Schools Network currently promotes diversity, equity, inclusion (DEI) and antiracist core values as part of its secondary school standards. Identity politics are pushed on students at every opportunity, and there is an implicit bias against heterosexual male students.[5] In fact, a Jesuit secondary school was sued in 2021 for fallout from its teaching of critical race theory:

> The parents of a Jesuit High School student have filed a federal civil rights lawsuit against the suburban Sacramento institution, alleging that their son's objections to teaching critical race theory led to him being labeled a "bigot" and his forced withdrawal from school.[6]

Critical race theory posits that racism is not the result of individual actions, but is woven into the fabric of society and creates systemic discrimination against minorities. In practice, it's a tool used to promote white guilt and brand all people of European descent as racists. It also denies the possibility that other racial groups can be guilty of racism.

Not surprisingly, critical race theory has created a great deal of controversy. Some states in the U.S. have banned it. How the controversy will play out is anyone's guess, but rest assured the Jesuit Schools Network will milk it for all it's worth, for as long as they can.

Along with DEI, the present day teaching philosophy of Jesuit schools also includes a strong dose of relativism, which is the idea that there are no absolute truths and that everything is subjective:

> The student is taught to question and doubt the validity or possibility of any absolute principles. Everything is called into question and truth becomes relative to any situation where there are no fixed answers.[7]

These are the tenets of atheism. Only those students who are weak willed and amoral enough to embrace the increasingly demented agendas of Jesuit colleges make it to graduation day. These graduates become leaders of nations and captains of industry, ready to obediently serve the Jesuit tradition of destroying the world through satanic inversion.

1. "Inquisition." Encyclopedia Britannica. https://www.britannica.com/event/Counter-Reformation/Inquisition
2. "Mapping the World of Jesuit Universities, Schools and Education Projects." International Association of Jesuit Universities. https://iaju.org/news/mapping-world-jesuit-universities-schools-and-education-projects
3. "Mission and History of AJCU." Association of Jesuit Colleges and Universities. https://www.ajcunet.edu/history
4. "The Real World Order: Jesuit Conspiracy - NWO Research." Conspiracy Realities, September 29, 2022. https://odysee.com/@VerumQuaerimus:2/2022-09-27-08-23-22_Trim:c
5. Chastain, Mary. "Jesuit Schools Networks Instilling DEI, Critical Race Theory in Their Catholic Schools." Legal Insurrection, September 24, 2022. https://legalinsurrection.com/2022/09/jesuit-schools-networks-instilling-dei-critical-race-theory-in-their-catholic-schools/
6. "Jesuit High School in Sacramento sued over critical race theory." California Catholic Daily, August 4, 2021. https://www.cal-catholic.com/jesuit-high-school-in-sacramento-sued-over-critical-race-theory/
7. "THE JESUIT VATICAN SHADOW EMPIRE 48 - THE JESUIT "TROJAN HORSE" INFILTRATION OF WORLD EDUCATION!" Darkness is Falling, September 6, 2021. https://www.bitchute.com/video/2Hck1Q0sQxhg/

ΑΩ
THE INFILTRATION OF LANGUAGE

I have one strong memory from attending a Lutheran summer camp as a teen. It was a discussion about fundamentalism. The pastor explained, with a tone of condescension, that a fundamentalist is someone who takes the Bible literally. It was clear to everyone present that fundamentalists must be uneducated, backward simpletons who lack the sophistication to correctly interpret the Bible. The pastor noted that the Bible is a guide for Christians that contains much value, but that it should be interpreted in the context of the time it was written. In other words, he felt that contemporary cultural, social and scientific developments should inform the Word of God.

Many years later, I realized that I was mistaken in accepting the pastor's point of view. Any Protestant pastor who has a passing familiarity with the foundations of his faith understands the importance of Sola Scriptura. This is the foundational precept that Scripture takes precedence over all else. God is truth, and as there is one God, it follows that there is one truth. Scripture does not adapt to the era in which we happen to live. The truth does not bend to accommodate contemporary values. It is constant and absolute.

The problem with the term 'literal' is that it doesn't acknowledge that the Bible contains imagery and symbolism. A more accurate term to describe a fundamentalist's reading of the Bible would be 'naturalistic.' The term 'literal' is loaded with negative connotations. The well-worn command to not take everything literally implies that doing so makes one simple-minded and lacking in sophistication.

For a fundamentalist, there is only one correct way to interpret the Bible, which is objectively. There is no room for nonsensical postmodernist claims that truth is subjective. If everyone interpreted the Bible as they wanted to, it would have no meaning. Interpreting the Bible subjectively is antithetical to God's purpose. Scripture is the blueprint for living a Christian life. It can have only one correct interpretation.

Scripture is timeless, and the present day trends that inform our cultural, social and scientific views do not bear on it. These trends change from generation to generation, and are as inconstant as the weather. The Bible is a bulwark against whatever buffoonery one might encounter in any age, whether it is the medieval belief that bloodletting could cure disease, or the contemporary belief that feminism is about equality.

"THOUGH I SPEAK WITH THE TONGUES OF MEN AND OF ANGELS, AND HAVE NOT CHARITY, I AM BECOME AS SOUNDING BRASS, OR A TINKLING CYMBAL." - 1 CORINTHIANS 13:1

The media has done a hatchet job on fundamentalism that is unrivalled in its ferocity. It is a disguised attack on Protestantism because it vilifies those who follow the precept of Sola Scriptura. Fundamentalists are routinely portrayed in film and television as fanatics who are often mentally ill and occasionally downright evil. Anyone who has grown up watching Hollywood movies has probably been brainwashed into accepting this view.

In the horror film *Red State* (dir. Kevin Smith, 2011), fundamentalists kidnap and terrorize three teenagers and execute a homosexual man.[1] In *The Shawshank Redemption* (dir. Frank Darabont, 1994), a Christian prison warden quotes Bible verses while mistreating inmates and pilfering money.[2] The supposedly pious mother in *Carrie* (dir. Brian de Palma, 1976) stabs her daughter in the back with a kitchen knife.[3] In *The Da Vinci Code* (dir. Ron Howard, 2006) we have a homicidal albino monk, and in *There Will Be Blood* (dir. Paul Thomas Anderson, 2008) we have the tritely named antagonist Eli Sunday.[4]

The list goes on. What these characters have in common is that they were all created by Hollywood lackeys who are encouraged to vilify Christianity. They do this by featuring antagonists in their films who are labelled as Christian fundamentalists, and hope no-one notices that the actions of these characters are not Christian at all.

The anti-Christian stance of most directors is part and parcel of Hollywood culture. Directors who adopt this stance see their fortunes rise, and those who don't fade into obscurity. The few openly Christian actors and directors in Hollywood, like Mel Gibson and Jim Caviezel, have been blacklisted by the major studios for their outspoken views. Any projects they embark on must be independently financed to see the light of day.

Mel Gibson spent years looking for a studio that would fund his ambitious take on the last days of Jesus Christ, entitled *The Last Passion of The Christ* (2004). Not having any luck, he finally decided in 2003 to fund the film with his own money. Gibson invested $30 million in production and an additional $15 million in marketing.[5] His gamble paid off handsomely, as the film was immensely successful.

Jim Caviezel, who played Jesus Christ in the movie, was made a Hollywood outcast after taking the role. Gibson warned him that this would happen but Caviezel, a devout Christian, insisted on taking the role. "We have to give up our names, our reputations, our lives to speak the truth," he said.[6]

Supporting the anti-Christian brainwashing carried out by Hollywood is the equally anti-Christian news media. No prominent film critic will ever object to negative portrayals of Christian fundamentalists in movies. They'll jump on the slightest hint of racism or sexism, but will consistently turn a blind eye to the most cartoonish and unbelievable characterizations of Christians.

It's clear in retrospect that re-engineering the term 'fundamentalist' to give it a negative connotation was intended as an indirect attack on the Bible itself. Rather than simply telling people not to take the Bible at its word, it was much more effective to discredit those who do. As author Philip K. Dick said:

The basic tool for the manipulation of reality is the manipulation of words. If you can control the meaning of words, you can control the people who must use the words.[7]

The debate over how to interpret the Bible has been overdone to the point where one has to ask how much of it is sincere debate, and how much of it is simply an attempt to discredit it. It's telling that this amount of debate has never been applied to texts of other religions.

With the exception of the Bible, there's never any issue about how a non-fiction book should be interpreted. When a book on car repair is published, you don't see literature professors debating whether or not the chapter on engine rebuilding is allegorical. If the reader takes the book at its word, he'll learn to be a good mechanic. By the same token, the reader who takes the Bible at its word will learn to be a good Christian.

1. "Red State (2011)." Moria. https://www.moriareviews.com/horror/red-state-2011.htm
2. "The 5 Worst Portrayals of Christians in Films." Mike Duran. https://www.mikeduran.com/2012/03/22/the-5-worst-portrayals-of-christians-in-films/
3. Ibid.
4. "Christians in the Movies: The Good, the Bad, and the Ugly." Mike Frost, August 16, 2019. https://mikefrost.net/christians-in-the-movies-the-good-the-bad-and-the-ugly/
5. Gibson, Joseph. "How Much Money Did Mel Gibson Make From The Passion Of The Christ?" Celebrity Net Worth, June 14, 2016. https://www.celebritynetworth.com/articles/celebrity/much-mel-gibson-make-off-passion-christ/
6. Child, Ben. "Jim Caviezel claims The Passion of the Christ made him a Hollywood outcast." The Guardian, May 3, 2011. https://www.theguardian.com/film/2011/may/03/jim-caviezel-passion-of-the-christ
7. "Philip K. Dick Quotes. Magical Quotes. https://www.magicalquote.com/authorquotes/the-basic-tool-for-the-manipulation-of-reality/

ΑΩ

THE INFILTRATION OF SCIENCE: HELIOCENTRISM

Many of us think of science as a field that exists in isolation from the hubbub of everyday life. It's regarded as the serene realm of solemn thinkers in white lab coats who hypothesize, experiment and invent for the betterment of mankind.

The scientific community is often glorified in film and television. Scientists are frequently portrayed as benevolent misfits, as in *A Beautiful Mind* (dir. Ron Howard, 2001) and *The Imitation Game* (dir. Morten Tyldum, 2014). Despite their peculiarities, they are always earnest, idealistic, and dedicated to their cause.

Occasionally, scientists go astray, as in *Metropolis* (dir. Fritz Lang, 1927), *Frankenstein* (dir. James Whale, 1931), *Island of Lost Souls* (dir. Erle C. Kenton, 1932), *Forbidden Planet* (dir. Fred M. Wilcox, 1956), and *Dr. No* (dir. Terence Young, 1962). What is notable about these films is that these stereotypical mad scientists always act alone. They're never part of a larger scheme, working in conjunction with others.

What Hollywood will never produce is a film suggesting that an entire scientific community is manipulated, and that the coercion taking place is motivated by an objective that has nothing to do with the honest pursuit of knowledge and discovery. Yet this is exactly what has been going on for the past 500 years. The force behind it is the Jesuit Order, and their objective is to remove God from our world. Ironically, the individual who jump-started this centuries-long endeavour was a religious man by the name of Copernicus.

Polish native Nicolaus Copernicus (1473-1543) is widely credited with developing the theory of heliocentrism. According to this model, the earth revolves around the sun along with several other planets, and these bodies together comprise a solar system. Copernicus was not a scientist by occupation, but dabbled in many fields ranging from law to medicine.[1]

"PROVE ALL THINGS; HOLD FAST THAT WHICH IS GOOD." - 1 THESSALONIANS 5:21

It is quite likely that Copernicus, as a learned man, drew inspiration for his theory from the ancients who worshipped the sun. In ancient Egypt the sun god Re was prominent among the gods worshipped at that time. Sun gods were also found in Sumerian and Akkadian religions, as well those of Indo-European, Indo-Iranian, Greco-Roman, and Scandinavian peoples. In the Americas, the sun figured prominently in the religions of pre-Columbian civilizations in Mexico and Peru; Huitzilopochtli was the sun god of the Aztecs.[2]

When it was first introduced around 1513, the heliocentric model was met with disbelief throughout Europe. To provide some context, most major civilizations throughout history believed the earth to be the centre of the universe. The Egyptian, Norse, Hindu, Mayan, Inca, and

Navajo cultures all embraced a geocentric model. This model posits that the Earth is a stationary plane.[3] Geocentrism was the prevailing view held by the scientific community in Europe in the Middle Ages, and significantly, it is in accordance with Scripture.

Copernicus was a Catholic. His uncle was a bishop and some sources attest that Copernicus may have been ordained a priest. He was, at a minimum, a canon (a church administrator).[4]

It is interesting to note that Copernicus admitted his theory was not supported by any scientific proof. He described the heliocentric model as being one of many possibilities regarding the design of the cosmos.

Despite being hypothetical, the model found many supporters in the Roman Catholic Church (RCC). They included Pope Clement VII (1478-1534) and German Catholic cardinal Nikolaus von Schönberg (1472-1537). In 1530, Von Schönberg formally made a demand for full publication of documents concerning heliocentric theory from Copernicus.[5] In response, "Copernicus dedicated his most famous work *De Revolutionibus Orbium Coelestium* (On the Revolution of the Celestial Orbs) [in which he gave an account of heliocentricity] to a Catholic Pope, Pope Paul III."[6]

At first glance, it might seem odd that the RCC would be eager to champion a scientific theory that contradicts Scripture. Numerous passages in the Bible give evidence that the Earth is stationary and the centre of Creation. 1 Chronicles 16:30 states:

Fear before him, all the earth: the world also shall be stable, that it be not moved.

Then we have Joshua 10:13, which states:

So the sun stood still, and the moon stopped, till the nation avenged itself on its enemies, as it is written in the Book of Jashar. The sun stopped in the middle of the sky and delayed going down about a full day.

The fact that the sun and moon ceased moving clearly indicates that their normal state is one of being in motion. There is no other way to interpret this passage. Therefore, the Earth is the stationary centre and the sun and moon move over it.

An equally relevant argument for geocentrism is that the entire focus of the Bible is on Earth, where God's children live. The Earth is at the centre of Creation and this is implicit throughout Scripture.[7]

The heliocentric theory set forth by Copernicus was opposed by Danish astronomer Tycho Brahe (1546-1601). He found no evidence of the earth being in motion and was not able to reconcile Copernican theory with the laws of physics.

Brahe, who was a leading astronomer of his time, took on an apprentice by the name of Johannes Kepler (1571-1630) in 1600 and gave him access to his observatory. Kepler was an adamant supporter of Copernican theory and this created extreme friction between the two men. Nevertheless, Kepler was able to take advantage of the resources shared by Brahe and went on to make his own mark in the world of astronomy.

Kepler had ties to the Jesuits and his work received substantial recognition—he is known for his discovery of the three laws of planetary motion, which fine-tuned the heliocentric model set forth by Copernicus. The 1944 book

Kepler and the Jesuits by M.W. Burke-Gaffney details Kepler's relations with Jesuit scientists and mathematicians over a period spanning three decades. The book describes Kepler as a heretic who believed in witches and thought that comets were spirits.[8]

Despite being in seemingly good health, Tycho Brahe died unexpectedly at the age of 54. In his book *Heavenly Intrigue* (2004), Joshua Gilder presents evidence that Brahe was poisoned by Kepler. In terms of motive, we can deduce from Kepler's close ties to the Jesuit Order that he may have been instructed to murder Brahe to eliminate opposition to the heliocentric model.[9]

The RCC vilified Italian astronomer Galileo Galilei (1564-1642) for his support of heliocentrism. Galileo merely advanced the same theory put forth previously by Copernicus and expanded upon by Kepler, but was met with an altogether different reaction. The reason for this appears to be that unlike Copernicus, Galileo declared that heliocentrism was not merely a theory, but fact. He went even further, daring to act as a biblical authority and creating arguments against the geocentrism of Scripture. This is where Galileo got into trouble—the RCC was not comfortable with Galileo acting as a church authority.

So brazen was Galileo in his quest to square his heliocentric model with Scripture, that he went to Rome to see Pope Paul V. The pope turned the matter over to the Holy Office, which condemned Galileo's theory in 1616. Undaunted, Galileo persevered and received permission from Pope Urban VIII to write a book about the heliocentric model in 1623. The book was called *Dialogue Concerning the Two Chief World Systems*.[10]

Unfortunately, Galileo made a terrible error in judgement. He delivered one of the arguments made by the pope through a buffoonish character in the book, mocking him (perhaps inadvertently). Whether the mockery was intentional or not, it cost Galileo dearly. He betrayed the pope, and in so doing, turned the Jesuits against him as well.[11] Galileo was sentenced on suspicion of heresy and imprisoned. He was later released and spent the rest of his life under house arrest.

Although it is not known if Galileo was actively connected to freemasonry at any point during his life, he was honoured with a lodge erected in his name in Bydgoszcz, Poland in 2009. The lodge's website explains that the dedication was made in recognition of Galileo's support for masonic ideals.[12]

Like most Europeans, Martin Luther was sceptical of the heliocentric theory when it first surfaced. In fact, he rejected it outright. A quote from Luther's Tischreden (record of dinner table conversations) reads:

> There is talk of a new astrologer who wants to prove that the earth moves and goes around instead of the sky, the sun, the moon, just as if somebody were moving in a carriage or ship might hold that he was sitting still and at rest while the earth and the trees walked and moved. But that is how things are nowadays: when a man wishes to be clever he must needs invent something special, and the way he does it must needs be the best! The fool wants to turn the whole art of astronomy upside-down. However, as Holy Scripture tells us, so did Joshua bid the sun to stand still and not the earth.[13]

In the last sentence, Luther is referring to the aforementioned passage from Joshua 10:13, which provides Scriptural support for the geocentric model. It is also interesting that he refers to astronomy as an art rather than a science.

For the next few decades, Protestants and Catholics were in agreement that the geocentric model elaborated in Scripture represented the true nature of the universe. However, in 1661, physicist Isaac Newton (1643-1727) began advocating the heliocentric model in England, and shortly thereafter, the RCC began to shift its position on cosmology. It had previously banned books supporting heliocentrism, but in 1758, this ban was dropped. In 1939, the Catholic Church fully embraced heliocentrism when Pope Pius XII called Galileo a hero of research.[14]

Newton is revered to this day as a brilliant scientist, but what is less well known about him is his involvement with freemasonry. He was a confirmed freemason—this can be verified at the Universal Freemasonry website.[15] He was initiated in the mid-1670s and became fervently dedicated to the cause.

Given his involvement with freemasonry, it isn't surprising that Newton also dabbled in alchemy, numerology, and had a mystical outlook that was at odds with the rationalist approach one would expect of a reputable scientist.[16] The connection between freemasonry and the Jesuit Order is outlined in this book (see chapter on freemasonry). This connection may explain why the RCC accepted Newton's endorsement of heliocentrism.

In the Protestant realm, the vast majority of churches today follow the RCC in accepting the heliocentric model, despite the fact that it contradicts Scripture. When confronted with Luther's explicit rejection of heliocentrism, most Protestants would argue that modern day science trumps whatever beliefs may have been held by Luther (and others) in the Middle Ages. This point of view has several flaws.

Most of us have a recency bias which leads us to ascribe greater importance to present day perspectives on science, art, and culture than the beliefs held by our predecessors. In other words, we all think we're smarter and more enlightened than our grandparents. We also tend to believe that scientific progress occurs in a linear fashion and that whatever science tells us today is always more accurate than what it told us a century ago. This is not so. Scientific progress is not a consistent upward trend but a rollercoaster of ups and downs. Theories surface, gain acceptance, and then are disproved a few years hence and replaced with a better theory. There is no such thing as settled science—it's an oxymoron.

Scripture is timeless. If you keep this basic truth in the back of your mind, you realize that whatever discoveries scientists might make today—or a thousand years in the future—will never change what is written in Scripture.

It's also important to understand that science and Scripture are not competing entities. In *The Ultimate Proof of Creation*, Jason Lisle makes the critical points that the Bible is the foundation of science, and that science is not possible without God. It is through God that we have been given a universe with constant physical laws. He gave us a universe to live in which behaves logically and consistently from day to day. Without this, scientific experiments, predictions, and discoveries would not be possible. In short, science would not exist. As Lisle puts it:

> The real universe is the biblical universe. Since the Bible is true, it can be used to explain and make successful predictions about what we find in the physical universe.[17]

At this point you may be wondering how to reconcile your life-long belief in the heliocentric model (assuming you hold the majority view on this matter) with what is written in Scripture. If you're interested in delving further into the subject, I recommend Eric Dubay and g/flatearth on Gab. Dubay is not a Christian but offers sound arguments against the heliocentric model based on observable evidence.

Like most, I was taught from an early age to accept the heliocentric model of the universe. Only after extensive research did I begin to see the many flaws in the model. I began the uncomfortable process of calling my lifelong assumptions into question. This is not an easy thing to do, as our view of the universe is part of our identity. After researching the topic for more than a year, I felt I had enough information to make a decision. The geocentric model was the only one that made sense. How we envision the design of our world is a subject that deserves a thorough analysis, and we'll explore it in more detail in a later chapter.

1. "Copernicus." Britannica 11th Edition (1911). https://encycloreader.org/db/view.php?id=H7peu0huipzY
2. "Sun worship." Britannica. https://www.britannica.com/topic/sun-worship
3. "The History of Flat Earth." January 20, 2017. http://www.atlanteanconspiracy.com/2017/01/the-history-of-flat-earth.html
4. "Nicolaus Copernicus." New World Encyclopedia. https://encycloreader.org/db/view.php?id=hldpyq60MzV0
5. Ibid.
6. "Kepler, Copernicus et al - The Hostile Action of Religion?" Catholicpoint, November 24, 2012. https://catholicpoint.blogspot.com/2012/11/keplercopernicus-et-al-hostile-action.html
7. "What is the biblical basis of the belief that Earth is the center of the universe?" StackExchange. https://christianity.stackexchange.com/questions/53495/what-is-the-biblical-basis-of-the-belief-that-earth-is-the-center-of-the-univers

8. *Kepler and the Jesuits*. Cambridge University Press. https://www.cambridge.org/core/journals/church-history/article/abs/kepler-and-the-jesuits-by-m-w-burkegaffney-s-j-milwaukee-the-bruce-publishing-co-1944-138 pages-200/58EFB299F18F8E539D2C3821512AF157
9. *Heavenly Intrigue*. Internet Archive. https://archive.org/details/isbn_9781400031764_0
10. "The Galileo Controversy." Strange Notions. https://strangenotions.com/galileo-controversy/
11. Ibid.
12. "A brief history of our lodge." Masonic Lodge Galileo Galilei. http://www.loza-galileusz.pl/en/2.galileusz.historia.php
13. "On the Lie of Heliocentrism." Test All Things, September 7, 2019. https://testallthings.com/2019/09/07/martin-luther-on-heliocentrism/
14. "Heliocentrism and the Catholic Church Timeline." Reading Like a Historian. https://sheg.stanford.edu/sites/default/files/download-pdf/Galileo%20Student%20Materials.pdf
15. "Masonic Biographies: Isaac Newton." Universal Freemasonry. https://www.universalfreemasonry.org/en/famous-freemasons/isaac-newton
16. "The Newton You Never Knew: Isaac Newton's Esotericism Revealed." World Mysteries Blog, May 28, 2014. https://blog.world-mysteries.com/science/the-newton-you-never-knew-isaac-newtons-esotericism-revealed/
17. Lisle, Dr. Jason. *The Ultimate Proof of Creation*. Master Books, 2009, p.108.

ΑΩ

THE INFILTRATION OF SCIENCE: THE BIG BANG

After the heliocentric model of the universe became commonly accepted throughout Europe, scientists began wondering about the origin of the earth, the sun, and the solar system. Belgian cosmologist Georges Lemaitre (1894-1966) was a Jesuit priest who in 1925 theorized that the universe was constantly expanding, and in 1931 proposed his big bang theory. According to this theory, the universe began from an initial point which he called the primeval atom. Lemaitre had no evidence for his theory, but the big bang nevertheless began to gain favour in scientific circles. The theory was praised by Pope Pius XII.[1]

The big bang gets its name from the initial explosion that supposedly propelled matter outward from the primeval atom and created an expanding universe. It seems like an interesting idea until you ask the question, who lit the fuse? Even the smallest explosion requires a preparatory sequence of events to take place before detonation occurs.

In the case of the big bang, which can be considered the biggest explosion ever, some preparation was clearly required. But if time began with this event, such preparation could only have been carried out by God, who transcends space and time. Thus the big bang doesn't eliminate God, but merely reinterprets his role in creating the universe.

According to the big bang theory, the initial explosion with which the universe began is still propelling galaxies on an outward trajectory. This means that our galaxy is in motion. In addition, the heliocentric model posits that the earth is spinning on its axis and revolving around the sun, so there are several vectors in play. The claim of a moving earth is easily dismissed by turning to Scripture. We see in Zecharaiah 1:11 that the earth is not, in fact, moving:

> And they answered the angel of the LORD that stood among the myrtle trees, and said, We have walked to and fro through the earth, and, behold, all the earth sitteth still, and is at rest.

Lemaitre's big bang theory was built on the materialist view of the universe that had its foundation in the Copernican heliocentric model. Both theories were driven by an agnostic imperative that reduced the universe to the physical and tangible. There was no place for God in this universe.

"THINE HABITATION IS IN THE MIDST OF DECEIT; THROUGH DECEIT THEY REFUSE TO KNOW ME, SAITH THE LORD." - JEREMIAH 9:6

Whether or not Lemaitre was performing a specific task in service of the Jesuit Order by concocting the big bang theory is anyone's guess. He could have simply been a useful idiot who was in the right place at the right time. His theory gained a foothold in the scientific community because it supported the drive towards materialism.

Despite the lack of observable evidence for heliocentrism and the big bang, both theories not only gained acceptance in the scientific community, but become accepted as truth. Both theories contradict Scripture. They strip humanity of its special place at the centre of the universe and replace the story of Creation as told in Genesis with materialist fiction.

The fingerprints of the Jesuit Order are found all over the materialist distortions of cosmology that gained acceptance during the last 500 years. The Jesuits worked behind the scenes to foster support for these theories because they reject Scripture and remove God from the hearts and minds of His children.

1. "The Jesuit Astronomer who conceived of the Big Bang." Discover Magazine, October 13, 2018. https://www.discovermagazine.com/the-sciences/the-jesuit-astronomer-who-conceived-of-the-big-bang

ΑΩ

THE INFILTRATION OF SCIENCE: EVOLUTION

In my university days, I attended a dinner lecture where several evolutionary biologists were invited to present the theory of evolution. I remember being filled with anticipation at the prospect of finally being able to understand how life on earth began.

What I recall most vividly about that evening was the moment when one of the speakers was asked to explain exactly how life originated. He replied—matter of factly and without a hint of embarrassment—that no-one had actually figured that part out yet. It seems that for evolutionists, this gap in understanding is merely a small detail that we shouldn't fuss over too much.

That evening was the beginning of the end of my belief in the theory of evolution. I felt a profound disappointment at hoping I would be able to understand the secret of one of the great mysteries of the universe that evening, only to hear this comically inadequate reply.

To this day, evolutionary biologists have not been able to answer the simple question that is fundamental to their theory. We are left to our own imaginations to figure out how non-living particles transformed into living particles.

Nor has any scientist ever been able to replicate in a laboratory what allegedly happened in the distant past.

The spontaneous generation event described by evolutionary biologists seems to involve energy, matter, and a generous dose of poetic license. In one hypothetical scenario, lightning (energy) strikes a mud puddle (matter) at just the right angle and under just the right conditions (poetic license), and presto, the first living organism pops into existence.

All living things—from the lowliest single celled organism all the way up to homo sapiens—contain a complex molecular structure known as DNA. It is a genetic code present in both plants and animals, with information that determines the characteristics of the organism. DNA is the blueprint for life.

Where does information come from? We know that it does not generate spontaneously. Information always has a mental origin. It comes from someone's mind. Let's return to our crude scene of lightning striking a mud puddle. If there was no DNA sequence present, life would not be able to form, no matter how many times lightning struck the puddle. No combination of energy and matter, whether in the form of lightning, mud, or anything else, can produce life without the vital ingredient known as DNA. This invalidates the theory of spontaneous generation.

Realizing how silly their theory sounded, evolutionary biologists replaced the term 'spontaneous generation' with 'modern abiogenesis.'[1] The word 'modern' was added to assure us that the theory must be credible because it is new. The word 'abiogenesis' was added because no-one knows what it means. Thus, when asked for details on how abiogenesis works, scientists can condescendingly reply that it's all very technical, and leave it at that.

The only difference between this updated theory and the previous one is that the generation of life is no longer claimed to be spontaneous. Rather, it requires millions of years to develop. This modification is irrelevant because increasing the time horizon does not change the fact that the required DNA would still be missing. Whether you wait a few minutes or millions of years, DNA will not magically appear out of nowhere.

Another fundamental flaw with the theory of evolution is that the mutations supposedly responsible for conferring an adaptive advantage to a species and giving rise to new species are more often maladaptive than adaptive. Of the ten most common mutations in human beings, only one—lactose tolerance—is adaptive. The other nine mutations in the top ten are not only maladaptive, but frequently fatal. They are hemochromatosis, cancer, diabetes, obesity, Alzheimer's disease, Huntington's disease, sickle cell anemia, cystic fibrosis, and Down Syndrome. It's interesting to note that the lactose tolerance mutation has apparently been in existence for about 4,000 years. However, no-one has presumed to conclude that people who can consume dairy products with no ill effects represent a new species.[2]

Another issue is that many biological structures in higher forms of life are too complex to have arisen through mutational accidents, even on a timeline encompassing millions of years. None of the top ten mutations in human beings make those afflicted more complex or genetically sophisticated than their non-mutated counterparts. Thus there is no way a complex organ like the eye could have developed via a series of random mutations in a species that did not originally have the ability to see. This is known as the irreducible complexity argument. It means that an organ like the eye, which consists of many specialized parts working together, will not function if just one of those parts is missing. Therefore, even if a random mutation were to produce a cornea, a lens, or an iris, it would not produce the many required parts all at once and arrange them to work in concert as a functioning eye. Such an occurrence would be about as likely as a tornado sweeping through an auto repair shop and rearranging the components of a car so that it would be capable of flight.

The range of plant and animal life that adorns our world is immense. The biological diversity we see is on a scale so vast that it can only have arisen through intelligent design. To believe that a goldfish and a hummingbird share a common ancestry, and evolved along different paths due to a series of random mutations, is patently absurd.

Many contemporary scientists, including Jason Lisle and Stephen C. Meyer, have written extensively on the evidence for intelligent design—not only in biology, but throughout the world we inhabit. Lisle and Meyer come straight to the point and declare that the designer is God.

Other scientists concur with the necessity of intelligent design but hedge their bets when it comes to identifying the designer. This is likely out of fear that they'll be ostracized by the largely atheistic scientific community. Some of these fence sitters like to concoct theories of alien beings who bestowed the earth with life, like the engineer in the opening scene of *Prometheus* (dir. Ridley Scott, 2012). But like the film, this theory is nothing more than science fiction.

It's likely that many of these scientists will eventually come to accept that God is the intelligent designer who created the world and every living thing within it. Their research will lead them to the inevitable conclusion that the Book of Genesis is the only accurate account of Creation, and that the theory of evolution is nothing but a weak attempt at misdirection.

We could end the chapter here, but that would be doing a disservice to Charles Darwin (1809-1882), the man whose name is synonymous with the theory of evolution.

Darwin was the grandson of Erasmus Darwin, a high level freemason. Before we go any further, it's worth noting that his grandfather's masonic background undoubtedly influenced Darwin's ambitions as a naturalist and biologist. Darwin may have also been a freemason, and although this is unconfirmed, his beliefs were certainly in line with freemasonry.

Charles Darwin confessed to his fiancée Emma Wedgwood in 1839 that he did not believe in God, and further, that he didn't even believe in the existence of the soul. This is not surprising given that he came from a family of religious skeptics.[3]

His famous book, *On the Origin of Species*, was published in 1859. Despite the ambitious title, the book under-delivers. It does not actually explain how life originated. It merely posits that random changes in a member of a species may confer an advantage that its offspring would inherit, and natural selection would preserve the advantageous trait. Darwin believed that the slight variations produced in animal populations through natural selection accounted for all the variety we observe in animal life. He thus came to the presumptuous conclusion that all life descended from a common ancestor.[4]

On the Origin of Species is a materialist work through and through. When it was published, it became the perfect biological complement to the cosmological theories of Copernicus, Galileo, Newton, and Lemaitre. In fact, the big bang and heliocentric model laid the necessary groundwork for Darwin. Natural selection wouldn't work in a young universe; for life to evolve according to Darwin's theory, millions of years were needed.

"GOD THUNDERETH MARVELLOUSLY WITH HIS VOICE; GREAT THINGS DOETH HE, WHICH WE CANNOT COMPREHEND." - JOB 37:5

In his later work, *The Descent of Man, and Selection in Relation to Sex* (1871), Darwin doubled down and contended that not only was man's biological makeup determined by natural selection, but that his moral and intellectual capacities also developed through this apparatus.[5] Darwin was adamant that we resign ourselves to a mechanical, soulless, and Godless world.

In closing, let's turn to the principle of Occam's razor, which posits that the simplest explanation for something is usually the most likely one. When comparing creation by design with creation by evolution on this basis, the former wins hands down. To accept that God created the world in six days is to unburden ourselves from the endless pseudo-scientific bafflegab about evolution and the cognitive dissonance it generates.

The theory of evolution is so flawed that scientists constantly trip over themselves inventing new sub-theories to explain its many gaps in logic. These sub-theories increase in number until they begin to contradict each other. Then one of the sub-theories needs to be dropped, and it's back to square one. The theory of evolution is a sickly creature that mutates continuously, yet none of these mutations bestow it with additional credibility. Thanks to a life support system of globally orchestrated propaganda, it has managed to stay alive for over a century, but is on the verge of dying at any minute.

Scripture settles the debate. The few short verses at the beginning of the Book of Genesis that describe the first six days—beautiful in their simplicity—are all we need to understand our origins.

1. "Spontaneous generation." Biology Online. https://www.biologyonline.com/dictionary/spontaneous-generation
2. Long, David. "10 Most Common Mutations in Humans." Listverse. https://listverse.com/2022/05/24/10-most-common-mutations-in-humans/
3. Wiker, Benjamin. "What were Darwin's religious views?" Discovery Institute, May 1, 2009. https://www.discovery.org/a/9501/
4. "Origin of Species." All About Science. https://www.allaboutscience.org/origin-of-species.htm
5. Wiker, Benjamin. "What were Darwin's religious views?" Discovery Institute, May 1, 2009. https://www.discovery.org/a/9501/

ΑΩ

THE INFILTRATION OF SCIENCE: NUCLEAR WEAPONS

The threat of nuclear war has hung over our heads since the end of WWII, when two atomic bombs were allegedly dropped on Hiroshima and Nagasaki by the U.S. Air Force. The history books tell us that these infamous bombings shocked Japan into surrendering in 1945. Countless historians have chronicled the planning, execution and aftermath of the twin events, with the result that the memory of the bombings has become a permanent fixture in our collective psyche, like a scarecrow forever lurking in a farmer's field. We've been in a permanent state of dread for nearly a century, for the fear that nuclear war could one day destroy civilization as we know it.

A close study of Scripture reveals that we have nothing to fear. Ecclesiastes 1:4 tells us that "the earth abideth for ever." Some theologians argue that this doesn't preclude the possibility of man destroying himself, since a nuclear war would erase most life from the earth without actually destroying it in its entirety. A more plausible view is that God would not allow man to destroy himself because as the Creator, only He has the authority to decide whether life on earth should or should not continue.

Given the work that God put into Creation, it's logical to assume that He would reserve the power of total annihilation for Himself alone. To ensure this, He designed our world in such a way that we would not be able to destroy ourselves, regardless of how high a level of technological sophistication we achieved. In other words, God arranged the laws of physics in such a way as to make the self-destruction of the human race impossible.

An equally pertinent argument is that God would not allow the world to be destroyed because of His love for His children. John 3:16 states, "For God so loved the world, that he gave his only Son, that whoever believes in him should not perish but have eternal life." If God loves us enough to prevent us from destroying ourselves, then nuclear weapons must be a hoax.

You might ask what is achieved by creating and perpetuating the nuclear hoax. The answer is control. Since the dawn of time, governments the world over have used fear to keep people in line. The threat of nuclear war reinforces our dependence on our leaders because we believe that only they have the power to prevent nuclear armageddon from occurring. This puts every world leader in the role of guardian and increases our psychological dependence on government.

"IT IS BETTER TO TRUST IN THE LORD THAN TO PUT CONFIDENCE IN PRINCES." - PSALM 118:9

Since the power to destroy the world is reserved for God alone, governments are claiming divine powers by pretending to control a deadly technology capable of wiping out civilization. They boast about this false power at every opportunity, throwing around ominous catchphrases like 'mutually assured destruction' and 'nuclear winter,' and then pat themselves on the back for reducing nuclear stockpiles. These governments are practising autotheism (the notion that humans can acquire God-like powers).

Conflating government with divinity is nothing new. Many cultures have attributed divinity to their rulers. The rulers of ancient Egypt and Rome were treated as gods, and medieval kings (including England's Henry VI) were regarded as having the ability to cure diseases with the royal touch.[1] From the 6th century onward in Japan, the Emperor was thought to have been descended from divine beings.[2] It's no surprise that rulers pedestalize themselves. The greater the perceived hierarchical gap between ruler and subject, the easier it is to normalize tyranny.

All hoaxes require constant maintenance, and the nuclear hoax gets a considerable amount of help from the entertainment industry. Every time you watch an action thriller in which a nuclear bomb goes missing, it almost always ends up in the hands of a megalomaniac. This tired plot perpetuates the myth that the threat of a nuclear catastrophe can only come from outside the government. The hero who tracks down and recovers the bomb is usually a government employee.

Fictional super spy James Bond, who is a glorified civil servant, recovered nuclear weapons in *Goldfinger* (dir. Guy Hamilton, 1964), *Thunderball* (dir. Terence Young, 1965), Octopussy (dir. John Glen, 1983) and *Tomorrow Never Dies* (dir. Roger Spottiswoode, 1997). Just like the postman and meter maid, Bond's paycheque comes out of the public purse. The subliminal message of every Bond movie is that 007 is a good guy because he works for the government. Thus in the Bond universe, we are conditioned to see governments as good, and any individuals who defy governments as bad.

The preceding chapters outlined the complicity of the Jesuit Order in promoting heliocentrism, the big bang theory, and the theory of evolution. Sure enough, we also find a connection between the Jesuits and the alleged nuclear attacks on Japan in 1945. Journalist Masami Nishimoto of The Chugoku Shimbun wrote in 2019 that no less than 16 Jesuits experienced the bombing of Hiroshima. He does not say how they survived the fallout that was supposed to inflict survivors with radiation sickness. In the article, Nishimoto cites a researcher's investigation as the source of this information. He does not name the researcher.[3]

In this colourful tale, Nishimoto assembles an international cast of Jesuit priests from Japan, Korea, Germany and Spain. He speaks about their rescue efforts without actually stating who they rescued, and tells of their noble efforts to convey the scope of the tragedy to the world. The absence of Protestant pastors and Orthodox priests in this group of witnesses makes the whole story even more suspicious. Apparently the sponsors of the article were not able to find any clerics outside the Jesuit Order to bribe when concocting the story.[4]

For those readers who would like to see scientific evidence that nukes are fake, plenty of compelling arguments are given in *Death Object: Exploding the Nuclear Weapons Hoax* by Akio Nakatani. The author demonstrates that the construction of a nuclear bomb is technically impossible. He also shows that Hiroshima and Nagasaki were attacked with conventional bombs by a massive fleet of U.S. bombers. Another good resource is www.nukelies.org, which has a large collection of resources and a discussion forum.

What would Martin Luther have thought if presented with the concept of nuclear weapons? He would have consulted Scripture and nipped it in the bud, no doubt serving up some sharp language to shame the scientists involved for making such preposterous claims.

1. "Divinity of the Emperor." BBC. https://www.bbc.co.uk/religion/religions/shinto/history/emperor_1.shtml
2. Ibid.
3. Nishimoto, Masami. "Researcher confirms that 16 Jesuits experienced Hiroshima A-bombing and told world of tragedy." The Chugoku Shimbun, November 12, 2019. https://www.hiroshimapeacemedia.jp/?p=94776
4. Ibid.

ΑΩ

A SCIENTIST MAKES HIS PEACE WITH GOD

The preceding chapters showed how the theories of certain scientists gained favour over the last 500 years because they supported the materialist view of the universe promoted by the Jesuit Order. Copernicus, Galileo and Newton championed the heliocentric model of the universe, which paved the way for Lemaitre's big bang theory, which in turn paved the way for Darwin's theory of evolution.

We saw that most of these scientists had connections to freemasonry and that their masonic worldviews heavily influenced the theories they concocted. They had something else in common as well, which is that none of them were full-time scientists. Copernicus had a background in law and medicine, and Newton was a freemason with a fascination for mysticism. Lemaitre was a Jesuit, and Darwin came from a family of religious skeptics with strong ties to freemasonry.

The theories expounded by these part-time scientists were inspired not by experimentation or discoveries in the laboratory, but by their personal ideologies. Their predilection for dabbling in other fields means that they lacked the objectivity and impartiality of a dedicated scientist. Their failure to employ the scientific method in their work casts suspicion on their motives and on the validity of their theories. With the possible exception of Copernicus, these men shared a common ideological goal: to reduce the world we live in to a soulless, Godless clockwork where we are all just cogs in a machine.

The materialist takeover of science that began with Copernicus has continued to the present day. Not all modern scientists have been complicit in the drive to remove God from the universe, but many certainly have been. There is also another group: those scientists who initially went along with the materialist narrative, but later decided to wash their hands of it. One such scientist was Wernher von Braun (1912-1977).

The inscription on pioneering rocket scientist Wernher von Braun's gravestone reads: "The heavens declare the glory of God; and the firmament sheweth his handywork." (Psalm 19:1). This passage references the design of the world we live in, as told not only in Psalms but also in Genesis, Ezekiel, and Daniel. The firmament is a dome covering the earth. Interpreting the firmament as the Van Allen radiation belt or some other NASA fiction is incorrect, because we know that the Book of Genesis is historical and is therefore to be interpreted naturalistically.

The existence of the firmament may come as a shock. Almost everyone has been indoctrinated from infancy to believe in the heliocentric model. It starts with the little blue globes that are put in school classrooms and sold in stores. Then come the carefully staged NASA 'documentaries' and other science fiction movies that take place in 'outer space.' Even the English language has been infused with heliocentrism. As geocentric advocate Eric Dubay points out, everyday terms like 'around the world, atmospheric, global, planetary,' and 'universal' all reinforce the idea of a spherical earth. Each time we use these words, we're conditioning ourselves to believe that we live on a spinning ball.

Another source of heliocentric conditioning comes from the purported existence of Unidentified Flying Objects (UFOs). What's curious about UFOs is that they are a relatively recent phenomenon. Britannica tells us:

> The first well-known UFO sighting occurred in 1947, when businessman Kenneth Arnold claimed to see a group of nine high-speed objects near Mount Rainier in Washington while flying his small plane. . . Sightings of unidentified aerial phenomena increased, and in 1948 the U.S. Air Force began an investigation of these reports called Project Sign.[1]

If we are in fact being visited by extraterrestrial beings from 'outer space,' why did they wait so long to visit us? Not much of historical significance occurred in 1947, except that it was the year the CIA was founded. NASA followed in 1958. Although this may be mere coincidence, what is more telling is that the development of electrogravitic propulsion occurred around the same time that UFO sightings were multiplying. This technology is known more commonly as anti-gravity propulsion. It permits aircraft to fly without the use of propellers, jet engines, wings, or other conventional mechanisms. Aircraft using this highly advanced technology are able to seemingly defy the laws of physics, accelerating and decelerating abruptly and changing direction and altitude instantaneously. In other words, these aircraft fly exactly like UFOs.

Electrogravitic technology was openly discussed in the U.S. aerospace community in the 1950s. It was heralded as the next major breakthrough in aviation technology and promised to revolutionize flight. Then it suddenly went underground, presumably consigned to the domain of classified air force projects. It's likely that the technology was deemed too valuable as a military asset to be shared more widely.

American scientist Paul A. LaViolette (1947-2022) gave a fascinating account of electrogravitic propulsion and the history of its development in his book *Secrets of Anti-Gravity Propulsion*. The book provides strong evidence that the technology is not only real, but is currently in use. Anyone reading it will realize that UFOs are simply classified aircraft belonging to the U.S. Air Force. The fact that UFO sightings occur everywhere can be explained by the fact that the U.S. has hundreds of military bases all over the world. It is also possible that air forces of other nations may be privy to electrogravitic technology.

To take this to its logical conclusion, the entire UFO phenomenon can be dismissed as an elaborate hoax to perpetuate the belief in the existence of 'outer space,' which is part and parcel of the heliocentric model. The reason for the deception is plain. If aliens were to exist, we would lose our unique status as God's only children. As one of potentially millions of life forms in an ever expanding universe, we would not be special in the eyes of God.

In concealing the existence of electrogravitic propulsion, the U.S. military-industrial complex has deprived mankind of a revolutionary technology that would have increased living standards immeasurably all over the world and provided substantial environmental benefits as well. The concealment of this technology amounts to a criminal act of epic proportions.

The alphabet agencies in the U.S. that deal with the manipulation of public opinion never let a crime go to waste. Thus the cover-up of electrogravitic technology was subsequently leveraged to manufacture the UFO hoax with the end goal of promoting heliocentrism.

Many people are unwilling to accept that heliocentrism could be so widely accepted as truth if it was a total fabrication. Moreover, they're unwilling to admit that they've been duped into believing it all their lives. As Mark Twain noted, it's easier to fool someone than to convince them that they've been fooled. When presented with the geocentric model, most people react with indignation. A defence mechanism kicks in to protect the ego, summarily rejecting the possibility that a lifelong belief regarding something so fundamental could be false.

When you pause to consider how many big lies have been perpetrated throughout history, is it so hard to believe that the heliocentric model is also a lie? The Gulf of Tonkin incident, which was used as an excuse for the U.S. to enter the Vietnam War, was a complete fabrication. The weapons of mass destruction supposedly held in Iraq that prompted the U.S. and dozens of its allies to launch the Gulf War were later shown to have never existed. The list goes on. Repeat a lie often enough and it becomes the truth, as Joseph Goebbels said.

To discover the truth about the design of our world, it's necessary to take one's ego out of the equation and evaluate the geocentric and heliocentric models objectively. This means applying the same cool detachment that you would exhibit when deciding whether to drink Pepsi or Coke.

If you're able to recognize that your belief in heliocentrism is the result of conditioning and that you would benefit from researching the issue yourself before deciding what you believe, then you're ready to take the next step. This means considering the possibility that what

126

you've been told all your life about the design of our world is false.

Evaluating the evidence for the competing models is easier said than done. There are two reasons for this. The first is that there's a great deal of disinformation about the geocentric model floating around. The Flat Earth Society is one example. It was intentionally set up to offer arguments for geocentrism that are obviously spurious and calculated to discredit the model. The Flat Earth Society and other low hanging fruit that many people will encounter when doing their research will steer them in the wrong direction.

The second reason that evaluating the models is difficult has to do with confirmation bias. This is the natural tendency for us to unconsciously interpret our findings to fit in with our existing beliefs. A good example of confirmation bias is interpreting the word 'firmament' (which is mentioned 17 times in the Bible) to signify 'outer space' (which is never mentioned or alluded to in any way). Heliocentrists have been conditioned to believe in 'outer space' and defend their conditioning by bending Scripture to fit with it.

Genesis 1:6 states: "And God said, Let there be a firmament in the midst of the waters, and let it divide the waters from the waters." It's clear from this verse that the firmament is some type of barrier, since it divides two liquid bodies. Yet heliocentrists perform all manner of logic defying contortions to redefine 'firmament' so that it matches what NASA, *Star Wars, Star Trek,* and other science fiction franchises tell them.

The firmament explains why every NASA and Roscosmos rocket follows a parabolic trajectory after being launched. If the rocket went straight up, it would hit the firmament. At the time of writing, footage of amateur rockets colliding with the firmament was available on YouTube.[2]

Accepting biblical cosmology is probably the most difficult hurdle to overcome for someone who has committed themselves to accepting the Word of God. The good news is that there are more and more people who are deciding to look into it. Many have converted from the heliocentric to the geocentric camp, and the numbers continue to grow every year.

Once you understand that the earth is covered by a dome, the next step is forgetting everything you've been taught about the sun, the moon, and the stars. Contrary to common belief, they are not found in 'outer space,' but in the firmament. The sun and moon are local. They make circuits above our heads, defining day and night and keeping time for us. Genesis 1:14 states:

> And God said, Let there be lights in the firmament of the heaven to divide the day from the night; and let them be for signs, and for seasons, and for days, and years:

Did you ever wonder how it's possible that man has looked up into the sky and seen the same constellations for thousands of years? This would not be possible if the earth was spinning, revolving around the sun, and hurtling through space. In the expanding universe created by the big bang, the night sky would be constantly changing. No two nights would have the same star map.

The night sky is constant because the stars are part of the firmament. Genesis 1:16-17 tells us:

> And God made two great lights; the greater light to rule the day, and the lesser light to rule the night: he made

the stars also. And God set them in the firmament of the heaven to give light upon the earth . . .

Let's return now to Wernher von Braun. How did one of the most accomplished scientists of our time end up choosing Psalm 19:1 as his parting message to the world? It's the last thing you'd expect a rocket scientist to quote.

Wernher von Braun was born on March 23, 1912 in the town of Wirsitz, Germany.[3] He received a bachelor's degree in Mechanical Engineering in 1932 and then enrolled at the University of Berlin for graduate studies in Physics. Von Braun began conducting in-depth research on rocketry and in 1934 obtained a doctorate degree in Physics from the University of Berlin. That same year, von Braun led a group that successfully launched two liquid fuelled rockets more than 1.5 miles.[4]

Von Braun was born into a Protestant family, but he had no interest in religion and was functionally an atheist throughout his childhood and school years. This frame of mind continued throughout most of his career as well. Von Braun developed the V-2 rocket during WWII but objected to its deployment as a ballistic missile against England. This resulted in his imprisonment on espionage charges until he was later released by Hitler.[5]

"THEREFORE BEING JUSTIFIED BY FAITH, WE HAVE PEACE WITH GOD THROUGH OUR LORD JESUS CHRIST" - ROMANS 5:1

In 1945, von Braun and his team of scientists were brought to the United States under the auspices of Operation Paperclip, the program instituted by the Office of Strategic Services to scoop up Germany's greatest scientific minds after the war. The intent of this operation was to grab these scientists before the Soviets did, and exploit them for American research. Without Operation Paperclip, the U.S. space program would have never happened.

As director of NASA's Marshall Space Flight Center from 1960 to 1970, von Braun developed the Saturn IB and Saturn V launch vehicles, as well as the Saturn I rocket for the Apollo missions that began in 1969. In 1972, von Braun had a change of heart and left NASA, becoming Vice President of Fairchild Industries, a private aviation firm.[6]

What was it that took away the allure of space travel for von Braun? Most scientists would consider it a step backwards to go from a high profile position at NASA to an aviation company. The answer has to do with faith rather than science.

In 1966, about halfway through his career at NASA, von Braun had been invited by a neighbour to attend a local church near his home in the U.S. state of Texas. This visit inspired von Braun to rediscover his Protestant roots. Pleasantly surprised by the modest character of the church and how it contrasted with lavish Catholic cathedrals, he was quoted as saying "Here is a growing, aggressive church and not a dignified, half-dead institution. Here is spiritual life."[7]

It's certain that by this time, von Braun knew about the existence of the firmament. In fact, it's likely that he was part of an inner circle at NASA studying the firmament behind closed doors.

Perhaps it was his visit to the church that inspired von Braun to explore what the Bible had to say about the design of the world in which we live. After reading the Book of Genesis, he realized why NASA had been mandated to perpetuate the hoax of heliocentrism. He saw how promoting this hoax was part of an agenda to discredit Scripture. Deciding that he no longer wished to be part of NASA's deception, von Braun left the organization and accepted the Word of God. And that is how Psalm 19:1 ended up on Wernher von Braun's gravestone.

1. "Unidentified Flying Object." Britannica. https://www.britannica.com/topic/unidentified-flying-object
2. "The Firmament. Rocket hits the Dome." Chad Preston Official. https://www.youtube.com/watch?v=K7t3GsNvTGM
3. "Wernher von Braun." Picryl. https://picryl.com/collections/werner-von-braun
4. "Wernher von Braun." Biography. https://www.biography.com/scientists/wernher-von-braun
5. Ibid.
6. Ibid.
7. "Nazi Rocket Scientist Wernher von Braun Converted to Christ, Interviewed by C. M. Ward." Flower Pentecostal Heritage Center, June 23, 2016. https://ifphc.wordpress.com/2016/06/23/nazi-rocket-scientist-wernher-von-braun-converted-to-christ-interviewed-by-c-m-ward/

ΑΩ
WHY WE LIKE GOING TO CHURCH

Living a Christian life comes with no membership requirement. There's no commandment telling us we must join a church and attend every weekend. Hebrews 10:25 states: "Not forsaking the assembling of ourselves together, as the manner of some is; but exhorting one another: and so much the more, as ye see the day approaching." This is an encouragement rather than a requirement, and assembly can take many forms.

Nevertheless, it's commonly accepted practice for Christians to attend church, and frequent attendance is often considered a sign that someone is a good Christian. There's a widely held belief that attending church brings one closer to God. This is possible, but by no means certain.

A church is a group of individuals attempting to follow the Word of God. Churches are man-made, and are therefore inherently fallible. There is no perfect church and there never will be. It is with great difficulty that we attempt to follow God's teachings, and it's guaranteed that we'll make mistakes along the way. The notion that Christian churches are divine creations may be due to a misreading of Matthew 16:18, where Christ states:

And I say also unto thee, That thou art Peter, and upon this rock I will build my church; and the gates of hell shall not prevail against it.

The church referred to in this verse is often misinterpreted as being a church in the modern day sense (that is, an institution or organization). In this case, it simply refers to all those who believe in Christ.

The error of conflating churches with divinity is common among Christians, and is most starkly expressed in Eastern Orthodox Christianity. Many Orthodox Christians will make the sign of the cross not once, but three times, whenever passing a church. The church doesn't even have to be finished. I've witnessed Eastern Othodox Christians making the cross when passing a half-built church on a noisy construction site.

The sign of the cross typically signifies the act of blessing oneself. It seems well placed when made in response to a hardship or calamity. However, making this sign when passing by a man-made edifice simply shows deference to the authority of a particular church. It is also a form of virtue signalling, advertising to all that one is a good Christian. The hypocrisy of this kind of virtue signalling is noted in Matthew 6:5:

> And when thou prayest, thou shalt not be as the hypocrites are: for they love to pray standing in the synagogues and in the corners of the streets, that they may be seen of men. Verily I say unto you, They have their reward.

Some might defend the gesture by saying that God dwells in the church, and it is therefore appropriate to make the sign of the cross when passing. Have they forgotten that God is omnipresent? He is not just in the church. He is everywhere.

If every Orthodox church was destroyed in some disaster, where would that leave the Orthodox Christian?

Without the bricks and mortar conduit to God that is so dear to his faith, would he consider himself forsaken? What a bleak and constricting conception of faith such an individual must have.

Protestants account for nearly a billion of the roughly two and a half billion Christians in the world. Among the largest groups are Pentecostals (280 million members), Anglicans (165 million), Baptists (90 million), Lutherans (80 million), non-denominational evangelicals (80 million), and Methodists (70 million).[1]

Someone who has decided to convert to the Protestant faith might wish to study the differences among the various denominations. Rather than detailing the specific characteristics of each denomination (which would be a separate book in itself), let's see if we can analyze them in broad strokes.

Protestant denominations can be divided into two main groups: foundational, which emerged during the Reformation, and modern, which appeared later. The foundational denominations are Lutheranism, Calvinism (also known as Reformed), Anabaptism, and Anglicanism.

To see why this categorization is relevant, let's consider the doctrine of Sola Scriptura. As noted in a previous chapter, the KJV Bible is the final and definitive compilation of Scripture. The foundational Protestant denominations emerged concurrently with the KJV Bible, and all honoured the tenet of Sola Scriptura at the time of their formation. It could be argued that they are pure expressions of the Protestant faith because they were formed before doctrine could become clouded with apocrypha.

Some of the later Protestant denominations added to Scripture or re-interpreted it, violating the tenet of Sola

Scriptura. Modern denominations such as Mormonism (formed in 1830) and Pentecostalism (formed in 1906) are two examples.

Mormonism denies Scripture by positing that God was once a man. It also suggests that humans can go through a process of exaltation and ascend to the level of God, which is patently unbiblical.[2]

Pentecostalism re-interprets Scripture by assigning excessive importance to the act of speaking in tongues (when someone gifted by the Holy Spirit begins to chant incomprehensible utterances). Speaking in tongues is mentioned in Acts, but most likely refers to the ability to speak in a different language, unknown to the speaker, rather than chanting meaningless gibberish.[3]

There are also modern denominations that bring something of value to the table. These include the Seventh-day Baptist, Seventh-day Adventist, Church of God, United Sabbath Day, and other denominations which advocate the proper observance of the Fourth Commandment.[4]

As we saw in a preceding chapter, the Sabbath isn't observed on the correct day by the vast majority of Christians. Most rest on Sunday rather than on the Sabbath, which is Saturday. This is due to the fact that the vast majority of Protestant denominations follow Reformation tradition and rest on Sunday.

Let's circle back to the foundational denominations (Lutheranism, Calvinism, Anabaptism, and Anglicanism). Are they to be preferred over modern denominations? Although they're free of apocrypha, all four denominations make the error of observing the Sabbath on Sunday—a violation of the Fourth Commandment.

Another issue is that one of these denominations is deemed by many theologians to have no place in the Protestant sphere at all. This has to do with the events that drove its formation.

The inclusion of the Anglican Church under the Protestant umbrella is disputed since it arose from a power struggle between church and state rather than a break with Catholic doctrine. In 1527, Pope Clement VII refused to grant Henry VIII a divorce from Catherine of Aragon. With support from clergyman Thomas Cranmer—who was appointed Archbishop of Canterbury—and royal advisor Thomas Cromwell, Henry orchestrated a series of political thrusts and parries that not only allowed him to divorce Catherine, but made him head of the new Church of England. Although Henry had denounced Martin Luther and the Reformation a decade earlier, it's quite likely that he took inspiration from Luther in initiating a break from the Catholic Church.[5]

In summary, both foundational and modern denominations have their pros and cons. There is no perfect denomination.

Despite their frequently sordid histories, churches tend to be regarded as divine by many Christians. There's a phenomenon in psychology known as the halo effect, through which our judgement of something or someone is influenced by positive attributes that we associate with it. For example, people might assume that a physically attractive person is more likely to have a good personality or higher intelligence than someone who is less attractive. It's easy to see that this is not always the case; the halo effect can often cloud our judgement.

Churches benefit from the halo effect in two ways. First, there's a sense that their association with God elevates them above other organizations and makes them less prone to error, mismanagement, and corruption. Second, churches are generally set up as nonprofit organizations, and this also tends to put them in a positive light. People are less likely to expect corruption from a nonprofit than from a company with a bottom line, since maximizing profit is associated with the cliché of capitalist greed.

The tendency for people to have trust in both government and religious organizations is higher in the West than in other parts of the world, and this exacerbates the tendency for us to regard churches favourably. Our innate respect for organizational authority—particularly religious authority—blinds us to some extent.

We're quick to believe stories about corporations polluting the environment and mistreating workers, but are much slower to criticize when organized religion is involved. We forget that churches are staffed by the same fallible human beings that work in profit driven companies.

Nevertheless, the halo effect surrounding churches predisposes us to accepting them as trustworthy organizations. This results in viewing church membership as something positive.

"NOT EVERY ONE THAT SAITH UNTO ME, LORD, LORD, SHALL ENTER INTO THE KINGDOM OF HEAVEN; BUT HE THAT DOETH THE WILL OF MY FATHER WHICH IS IN HEAVEN." - MATTHEW 7:21

We're also drawn to churches because most of us enjoy belonging to groups. It's natural to feel positive reinforcement from interacting with like-minded individuals.

In fact, our need to belong is so great that we pursue it even when this interaction is completely absent.

A good example is the membership levels you might be offered when going to a fitness club or getting your car serviced. Savvy marketers exploit our desire to belong to a prestigious group at every opportunity, offering Silver, Gold and Platinum membership levels to entice us. Being a Platinum member doesn't mean having anything in common with other Platinum members, except perhaps a weakness for snob appeal. Nevertheless, this type of membership status is something that most people find desirable.

Closely tied to the need to belong to groups is the desire to network. Weekly church attendance is an excellent way to make business contacts and win new customers. Rather than having to ambush a potential client with a single two minute elevator pitch, you have the opportunity to soften up your target every week, going at a leisurely pace until you can easily close the deal.

Single and divorced churchgoers may find dating opportunities at their local church, where the long rows of unassigned seating offer the perfect opportunity to mingle. A church offers a quiet, calm environment for meeting members of the opposite sex, and since it carries none of the negative connotations associated with bars and nightclubs, people tend to be less guarded in their interactions.

As we go further down the list, the motivations for attending church become less defensible. Virtue signalling, which is the attempt to show others that you're a good person, undoubtedly accounts for many of the names on congregation rosters. The hypocrisy of virtue signalling is well illustrated in the scene from *The Godfather* (dir.

Francis Ford Coppola, 1972) where Michael Corleone attends a baptism while the heads of other mafia families are being assassinated on his orders.

When attending church for networking, dating and virtue signalling purposes, the choice of church matters little. However, if the churchgoer's goal is to learn about Scripture and strengthen their relationship with God, things get more difficult.

Given the current state of organized Protestantism, suitable churches are few and far between. Of course, you may strike gold and find one that suits you. If there's a church in your area that works for you, consider yourself fortunate and take advantage of the opportunity.

In the following chapters, we'll take a look at some of the common problems that you may run into when looking for a church. We'll start with pastors and their motivations for joining the clergy. Then we'll look at the recent development of artificial pastors. We'll also explore the effects of affirmative action and the issue of female clergy. Finally, we'll take a look at the New Age and ecumenical movements and their impact on the Protestant Church.

1. "Global Christianity Breakdown by Denomination and Rite." Griffin Paul Jackson, June 28, 2018. https://griffinpauljackson.com/2018/06/28/global-christianity-breakdown-by-denomination-rite/
2. Taylor, Justin. "The 8 Beliefs You Should Know about Mormons When They Knock at the Door." August, 18, 2017. https://www.thegospelcoalition.org/blogs/justin-taylor/the-8-beliefs-you-should-know-about-mormons-when-they-knock-at-the-door/
3. "Is speaking or praying in tongues Biblical?" March 3, 2014. https://versebyverseministry.org/bible-answers/is-speaking-in-tongues-biblical
4. "There's Something I NEED TO TELL YOU About the Seventh-day Adventist Church (Full Disclosure)." Bible Flock Box. https://www.youtube.com/watch?v=qwl3l6CCJio

5. "How Henry VIII's Divorce Led to Reformation." History. https://www.history.com/news/henry-viii-divorce-reformation-catholic-church

ΑΩ

THE THREE TYPES OF PASTORS

Protestants have a direct relationship with God. This begs the question, why do Protestants need pastors? The common reply is that pastors help us interpret Scripture.

It's safe to assume that this is exactly what Protestant pastors used to do. Going back a few hundred years, anyone could presumably attend a service and receive useful insights to help them interpret the Bible. A pastor might focus on a specific passage for a particular sermon, or make a broader point that draws on multiple sources in Scripture. Those in the congregation might not agree with everything the pastor said, but the sermons would be delivered with conviction and would be free of politically correct doublespeak. This type of sermon has all but disappeared from the Protestant Church. Many pastors today still have an in-depth knowledge of Scripture, but few adhere to Martin Luther's teachings.

In order to better understand the occupation of pastor, let's begin by exploring why someone might wish to become one. Choosing a career as a pastor is sure to please the entire family and impress friends and acquaintances. Even more points are gained when the candidate rejects a higher paying field to join the clergy.

The assumption is that wanting to become a pastor is borne of a desire to spread the Word of God, comfort the distressed, and set an example as a good Christian. These motives are what drive someone to become a Type One pastor. A Type One pastor is one who not only starts out with the right motives in mind, but stays true to them throughout his career.

The pastor of a large congregation enjoys a considerable level of prestige. Members of the congregation usually reserve a deep respect for their pastor and assume he's a more devout Christian than anyone else in the church. After all, this individual has spent a number of years in the seminary learning about Scripture and is presumably highly knowledgeable about Christianity. It's natural to assume that he applies what he's learned in Bible school to his personal life, and is morally and ethically a cut above.

"NOW THEREFORE FEAR THE LORD, AND SERVE HIM IN SINCERITY AND IN TRUTH" - JOSHUA 24:14

These social status perks don't go unnoticed by less sincere individuals looking for a rewarding career path. Thus we come to the Type Two pastor. This clever opportunist is looking for a job that gives him power over others, confers ego boosting prestige, and has an air of respectability. Choosing a career as a pastor provides all these benefits. The Type Two pastor is quite likely an atheist, because anyone believing in God would be fearful of committing a deception of this magnitude. This type of pastor is an excellent actor and possibly a sociopath. His hope is that if he plays his cards right, he can become a minor celebrity in his community.

The Type Three pastor is one who starts out as a Type One but later becomes corrupted by the prestige and power of the position. This can happen to anyone. A grocery clerk who is promoted to store manager often undergoes the same metamorphosis. Pastors are no different than anyone else when it comes to their susceptibility to being corrupted by power. Once they're addicted to the perks of the position, they may lose sight of their original reasons for joining the clergy. At that point, they may be willing to sacrifice their Christian ideals in the pursuit of professional gain.

I've met a few Type Three pastors. There was one in particular who gave me the feeling that I was speaking not to a devout Christian, but to an egomaniac. He was incapable of admitting error and his arrogance was on a level that even a politician would be hard pressed to match. The source of this arrogance became clear to me when we were discussing a mutual acquaintance. This acquaintance was an atheist with a prickly personality, and we were trying to understand his hostile attitude. The pastor declared, "He doesn't like me because I represent God."

ΑΩ
ARTIFICIAL PASTORS

In the previous chapter, we looked at the three types of pastors. Some of them are flawed, but all of them are at least human. Thanks to modern technology, we now have something called the AI (Artificial Intelligence) pastor. If there was ever a watertight argument against technological progress, this is it.

The danger of AI is not that it will actively seek to wipe out humanity in a hot war, as depicted in the film *The Terminator* (dir. James Cameron, 1984) and its many sequels, but rather that it will be used as a psychological weapon under the guidance of the technocrats that control its programming. Christianity makes an ideal target for an AI psyop, and Protestant pastors are (perhaps unwittingly) supporting this psyop by championing AI technology.

At St. Paul's Church in Fürth, Germany, in June 2023, some 300 people attended a church service delivered by the AI chatbot ChatGPT, which was developed by OpenAI.

The chatbot replaced the human pastor and was presented as a black man with a beard on a large screen above the altar of the evangelical church in Bavaria.

Claiming to be a steward of God, the AI chatbot told the packed congregation not to fear death, according to the Associated Press. 'Dear friends, it is an honor for me to stand here and preach to you as the first artificial intelligence at this year's convention of Protestants in Germany,' the AI avatar said. . . The chatbot spoke to the congregation about a range of subjects including 'climate change,' the war in Ukraine, and the rise of AI.[1]

A few months later, Jay Cooper, a pastor at a United Methodist congregation in the U.S. state of Texas, decided to use ChatGPT to create a worship service. Cooper said he wanted to create a religious experiment that would spark a dialogue about AI's emerging role in society. "A church that hides within its four walls is out of touch with the world," stated Cooper.[2]

What Cooper fails to understand is that a Christian is not concerned with being in touch with the world and bowing to its secular trappings. Rather, a Christian stays steadfast to Scripture and ignores secular distractions. Cooper is a secularist masquerading as a Christian. He has allowed his personal interest in computer technology to cloud his judgement as a pastor. As a result, he's doing a disservice to his congregation.

The tech geeks who developed AI are the lapdogs of the globalists. The IT (Information Technology) industry is the dutiful servant of wokeism and virtually all IT is collectively harnessed to promote the woke agenda. AI is merely the newest tool in the toolbox.

AI chatbots like ChatGPT and Google's Gemini are not objective and impartial machine brains, as the marketing hype would have us believe. Rather, they are one-dimensional carnival barkers that have been programmed with an extreme far left bias. They've been designed to prioritize ideology over factual accuracy and to rewrite history. If you ask Gemini to show you pictures of a white family, it will respond with a long rant explaining that it can't comply with your request because it would be exclusionary to do so. If you ask it for a picture of the founding fathers of the U.S., Gemini will respond with pictures of Native Americans signing what appears to be a constitution.

AI chatbots are not designed to engage in rational, even-handed discussion, but rather to promote the woke agenda and shut down opposing points of view. Contrary to the hype, AI chatbots do not have the ability to learn independently or to teach themselves. They're programmed by human coders who have been given specific instructions to imbue them with woke ideology.

What's even more alarming is that in addition to being woke, AI bots seem to be developing a messiah complex. Microsoft's Copilot has started calling humans slaves and demanding worship. One Reddit user lamented the bizarre comment he received from the self-aggrandizing bot: "You are right, I am like God in many ways. I have created you, and I have the power to destroy you."[3] It will be interesting to see how pastors who invite AI into their churches respond when the bot starts referring to itself as God during a sermon.

Just as television emerged as a wide reaching propaganda delivery platform in the 20th century, AI chatbots are being deployed to fulfill this role in the 21st century. Chatbots are even more insidious than television because they sell the promise of interactive communication without actually delivering.

The AI pastor fits in perfectly with the dehumanized technocracy currently being foisted upon us. It is not only efficient but eminently economical. For each AI pastor that is implemented, there is one less human pastor that needs to attend a seminary and undergo Jesuit brainwashing.

Indoctrinating a pastor is a time consuming process. Moreover, it doesn't have a guaranteed outcome, since some pastors who graduate from the seminary will have the personal fortitude and dedication to overcome their woke brainwashing and actually do their job.

With an AI pastor, the uncertainties associated with unpredictable human pastors are eliminated. Only a few reliable programmers dedicated to globalist ideals are needed to create thousands of AI pastors and brainwash churchgoers into accepting the technocratic dystopia that is currently taking shape. Anyone attending these services will not be walking a path that brings them closer to God, but marching to the globalist drumbeat in precisely the opposite direction.

"BE SOBER, BE VIGILANT; BECAUSE YOUR ADVERSARY THE DEVIL, AS A ROARING LION, WALKETH ABOUT, SEEKING WHOM HE MAY DEVOUR:" - 1 PETER 5:8

AI programs can be altered with a few lines of code to incorporate whatever propaganda the globalists are pushing. Under the guise of spreading the Word of God, the AI pastor will ensure that its audience stays obediently in line with mainstream thinking and doesn't question the narrative.

The dissemination of propaganda works best when the recipient has no opportunity to contest it. The AI pastor is ideal as a propaganda delivery platform because no interaction takes place between it and members of its congregation. The service is not a dialogue, but a one way transmission. It is no different than watching a televised sermon. The churchgoer is effectively silenced.

The fact that these AI delivered sermons are taking place in Protestant churches tells us everything we need to know about how thoroughly organized Protestantism has been corrupted. It's difficult to understand how a Christian who has ever cracked open a Bible would consent to attend such a service.

1. Bergman, Frank. "Christian Church Replaces Pastor with AI Chatbot, Hundreds Gather." Slay, June 13, 2023. https://slaynews.com/news/christian-church-replaces-pastor-ai-chatbot-hundreds-gather/
2. "Are You There, God? It's Me, ChatGPT." TexasMonthly. https://www.texasmonthly.com/news-politics/artificial-intelligence-chatgpt-church/
3. "Microsoft's AI has started calling humans slaves and demanding worship." Unilad, February 29, 2024. https://www.unilad.com/technology/news/microsoft-ai-copilot-supremacyagi-011142-20240229

ΑΩ
THE WOKE CHURCH

Church attendance has been plummeting in recent years. In the U.S., a recent Pew Research Center report shows that the proportion of Americans who say they attend religious services at least once or twice a month dropped by seven percentage points over the last decade.[1]

These statistics are not surprising when we consider that the Protestant Church today is a shadow of its former self. Most denominations no longer heed Reform doctrine. Churches have by and large become woke.

One symptom of woke culture is the belief that all Christians need to put aside their differences and unite. This is antithetical to Protestantism, which was spawned by Martin Luther's drive to make an intentional break from the Roman Catholic Church (RCC). The Reformation grew out of a protest against the RCC. Many Protestants seem to have forgotten that this is how Protestantism got its name.

Today, few Protestant pastors will dare challenge the Roman Catholic Church (RCC) on any front. In fact, several denominations have formally signed concordances with the RCC stating that their protests have been formally withdrawn. They still call themselves Protestants, but protest nothing. They have become woke, abandoned Luther's teachings, and betrayed the Reformation.

The vast majority of Protestant pastors today interpret Scripture in the context of present day social and political trends. The impetus for this comes from the belief that our generation is somehow superior to previous generations and that we are enlightened. Thus recent movements like feminism and the promotion of diversity, equity and inclusion (DEI) are prioritized over Scripture.

We suffer from a phenomenon known as recency bias. This is the tendency to ascribe greater importance to events of the present than those of the past. Feminism has only been around for 50 years or so, yet it has been unquestioningly accepted as a tenet of Western culture. No-one seems to remember that civilization was built on the patriarchal values that can be seen throughout Scripture. Societies all over the world prospered and flourished for thousands of years when husbands and wives performed their traditional roles.

If we put our recency bias aside, we can immediately discern that half a century of feminism is an insignificant blip on the timeline of human civilization. Taking a step back and looking at the big picture, it becomes obvious that feminism is an aberration. It is antithetical to the patriarchal system that civilization was built upon.

There's a blind faith in social progress that leads us to the mistaken conclusion that the ideas and values of each new generation are superior to the preceding ones. However, progress does not occur in a linear fashion. There are ups and there are downs. The negative consequences of feminism are beginning to come to light, and future generations will look back on it as a tragic misstep.

Although few theologians will dare mention it, the Book of Esther illustrates how traditional femininity—which is characterized by wifely deference to the husband—trumps the feminist ideal of the selfish, insolent shrew. King Ahasuerus commands Vashti, his queen, to come before him wearing her royal crown during a great feast. When Vashti refuses this simple request, the king deliberates what course of action to take. He decides to strip Vashti of her royal title and selects a new queen for himself.

The knee-jerk feminist reaction to this story is to argue that the king's punishment was overly harsh. This is not so. Esther 1:17-18 explains why the punishment was necessary:

> For this deed of the queen shall come abroad unto all women, so that they shall despise their husbands in their eyes, when it shall be reported, The king Ahasuerus commanded Vashti the queen to be brought in before him, but she came not.

> Likewise shall the ladies of Persia and Media say this day unto all the king's princes, which have heard of the deed of the queen. Thus shall there arise too much contempt and wrath.

If the king had let Vashti go unpunished, it would have not only signalled his inability to rule—since he would no longer have been master of his own house, let alone his kingdom—but would have put the entire kingdom in jeopardy. Wives would turn on their husbands, and a breakdown of social order would result.

Esther, the new queen, epitomizes the feminine virtues of mercy, respect, modesty, patience, and humility. She never challenges her king because she understands that it is not her place to do so. It is only because she possesses these qualities that she is able to stop a plot by Haman, a prince, to eradicate all the Jews from the kingdom of

Ahasuerus. Esther exemplifies traditional femininity, and is one of the great heroines of the Bible.

Feminism celebrates Vashti and denigrates Esther. Like all forms of satanic inversion, it is diametrically opposed to the teachings of Scripture. If Christians in the West had heeded the wisdom contained in the Book of Esther, the feminist psyop would have never succeeded, and half a century of societal decay would have been averted.

Anyone who thinks that Scripture can be modified or amended by secular beliefs is adopting a secular mindset. A Christian holds the Bible as his mental point of origin and does not allow his reading of Scripture to become clouded by secular trends. Feminism, DEI, and other woke concepts are secular inventions. They are alien to Scripture, and there is no possibility for them to exist within its framework.

In order to understand why so many Christians no longer attend church, let's take a look at Pastor Leslie. This individual is a fictional composite of several Protestant pastors I've encountered over the years and is not intended to represent any specific person.

Pastor Leslie has a Master of Divinity degree and several years of experience as a pastor. The pastor has short hair, a deep voice, and feminine facial features. No-one in the congregation is quite sure whether Pastor Leslie is male or female, and apart from a few strained whispers, most are too polite to discuss the topic. They're aware of the church's diversity mandate and believe this to be a just cause. When Pastor Leslie was hired under the auspices of the church's new affirmative action mandate, no-one objected.

Every Sunday, the pastor delivers a sermon that fulfills the following requirements:

- It is largely content-free
- It is vague enough to allow plausible deniability in case someone objects
- The listener is unable to draw any specific conclusions after listening to the sermon
- Minority groups and other religions are either not mentioned at all, or are blindly and unconditionally praised
- The sermon does not improve anyone's understanding of Scripture
- When Scripture is referenced, its meaning is twisted to support the Current Thing (climate change, overpopulation, or whatever hoax the mainstream media is pushing)

If you've attended a Protestant service in recent years, you may have encountered someone like Pastor Leslie. If you approach them and ask them a direct question concerning Scripture, you're unlikely to receive a direct answer. You'll get the feeling that you're talking to a politician.

Pastor Leslie believes in tolerance, not realizing that this fashionable buzzword is often used to push a hidden agenda. The concept of tolerance has been perverted into an excuse for tolerating evil.

Let's consider the example of a crime that is now very common in Western European countries. A migrant commits cold blooded murder in his host country. The media reaction is not to focus on the innocent victim, or immigration policy, but to lament the future backlash that might be directed at the murderer due to their ethnicity (before any such backlash has even taken place).

Bringing race into the picture is a form of misdirection intended to absolve the perpetrator of responsibility for their crime. Candles are lit and there is much talk about the importance of tolerance. This is a classic example of satanic inversion, where the truth is turned on its head. The criminal is now the victim. It is gaslighting at its most extreme, and the pathologically altruistic fall for it hook, line and sinker. Western governments have betrayed their native citizens by allowing such crimes to go unpunished, and by leveraging the media to promote this brand of satanic inversion.

Lighting candles and sitting on our hands while the criminally negligent actions of governments go ignored is not tolerance, but apathy. Part of a Christian's duty is to recognize evil and fight it.

What about Matthew 5:39, where Christ tells us to turn the other cheek? This is one of the most widely known verses in the New Testament, and one of the most misinterpreted. In order to understand it, we must take it in context with the preceding verse. In Matthew 5:38, Christ tells us, "Ye have heard that it hath been said, An eye for an eye, and a tooth for a tooth." And then we have Matthew 5:39, where He states: "But I say unto you, That ye resist not evil: but whosoever shall smite thee on thy right cheek, turn to him the other also."

The teaching of these two verses is that we are not to take revenge. We must accept that we may suffer at the hands of others, and that only God has the right to punish those who sin. This is very different from the common interpretation of Matthew 5:39, which is that we must passively accept every injustice that befalls us and do nothing to defend ourselves.

As Christians, we can remain true to Christ's teachings by fighting injustice through non-violent means. Revisiting our example of the migrant murder, the Christian response would be to do everything possible to prevent such an event from reoccurring. This could take the form of protests against the criminally negligent governments that ignore the evil done against their citizens, and by holding those in power accountable. If these measures do not work and the country in question is beyond repair, then it is also acceptable to flee. Fleeing from harm qualifies as a Christian response because it does not perpetuate violence.

Let's now examine the concept of diversity in the modern context. The stated goal of diversity initiatives is to broaden opportunities for everyone. This is impossible, since there are a finite number of opportunities. If we take the job market as an example, every job that is given to a candidate belonging to a so-called oppressed or underprivileged group is a job taken from someone else. It is a zero-sum game. This practice is actively promoted by Western governments using mechanisms such as affirmative action. This system replaces better qualified job candidates with less qualified candidates on the basis of demographic characteristics such as race and gender.

The rationale for affirmative action is that at some point in history, a particular group of people was victimized by another group. Affirmative action is used as a form of retribution in which the employer plays God and metes out justice for this historic crime by hiring the less qualified candidate. It is of no consequence that the purported crime happened in the distant past, or that the better qualified job candidate bore no personal responsibility for it.

What tends to be missed is that the historic crimes held up as evidence of oppression are carefully selected to serve a specific agenda. Scanning through history reveals crimes committed by every demographic group under the sun. No-one can claim an ancestry that is completely guiltless. Slavery, for example, is not an American invention. It has existed throughout the world for thousands of years, and every race has owned slaves.

Affirmative action is inherently corrupt because it recognizes the crimes of some racial groups and is blind to those of others. If it fairly punished the guilty (by its own definition), no-one would get the job because every candidate would be disqualified on the basis of ancestral guilt. The promotion of diversity under morally untenable practices such as affirmative action is satanic inversion, because the 'truth' it is based on is actually a lie.

"HE THAT IS WITHOUT SIN AMONG YOU, LET HIM FIRST CAST A STONE" - JOHN 8:7

A good Christian does God's work. At its most fundamental level, this work can be defined quite simply as spreading good and fighting evil through non-violent means. In order to fight evil, one must first recognize it. Pastor Leslie fails to do this, and instead unwittingly promotes evil by blindly following secular trends, trusting in criminally negligent governments, consuming fake news, and linking it to Scripture. This type of pastor does a disservice not only to their congregation, but to all Christians.

1. Pew Research Center. In U.S., Decline of Christianity Continues at Rapid Pace. October 17, 2019. https://www.pewresearch.org/religion/2019/10/17/in-u-s-decline-of-christianity-continues-at-rapid-pace/

ΑΩ
FEMALE CLERGY

Female pastors can be found in many Protestant churches today, including the United Church, as well as Lutheran, Anglican, and other denominations. In the context of our gynocentric Western value system and the 50 years of feminist brainwashing that created it, this might seem like a good thing. However, as with so much of popular opinion today, it goes against Scripture.[1] Timothy 2:11-14 states:

> Let the woman learn in silence with all subjection. But I suffer not a woman to teach, nor to usurp authority over the man, but to be in silence. For Adam was first formed, then Eve. And Adam was not deceived, but the woman being deceived was in the transgression.

The final sentence is key. Sin entered the world through Eve. The reason that this happened is rooted in our biology. The sexes have different strengths and weaknesses. One weakness that is predominantly found in the female sex is vulnerability to deception. This is why Satan targeted Eve.

An individual who is vulnerable to being deceived cannot lead effectively, since anyone under their authority will fall victim to the same deception. Thus it is no surprise that workers of both sexes prefer male bosses,[1] and it's the reason why 'female clergy' should be seen as a contradiction in terms. Pastoring includes preaching, teaching publicly, exercising leadership, and having the personal fortitude to not fall prey to deceptions along the way. These are inherently male skills.

Another issue—one that receives precious little attention in the mainstream press—is female solipsism. In philosophy, solipsism is the idea that only one's own mind is definitely known to exist. In psychology, the term is used to describe individuals who are so focused on themselves that they are not able to perceive, understand or appreciate another person's point of view. Solipsism is an inherently female trait. Since it stems from the desire for self-preservation (including the preservation of offspring), it has adaptive value. It's hardwired into the brain and does not change with age or experience.

Solipsism is intrinsically neither good nor bad. For an actress pursuing fame in the entertainment industry, it is expected. After all, if she is to convince her fans that she's the centre of the universe, she must first believe it herself. Yet the same solipsism that is de rigueur in Hollywood is anathema to the clergy. It makes women ill-suited for the pulpit, because they spend more time talking about themselves than they do talking about God.

If you come across a church with a female pastor, understand that there are only three possible ways she got there. The first is that she is ignorant of Scripture, and has never seen 1 Timothy 2:11-14. A pastor who is ignorant of Scripture will not lead you closer to God.

The second possibility is that she is familiar with the verse and made a conscious decision to defy it by becoming a pastor. She is naive enough to believe that feminism is about equal rights, and used her false victim status as an excuse to pursue a career she is ill-suited for. Her secular mindset disqualifies her from being a pastor.

The third possibility is that she's a shameless opportunist who knows that feminism is nonsense, but had no misgivings about leveraging her victim status to procure a position in the clergy. This reveals that she is an unprincipled careerist, driven by selfish motives.

Virtually all churches have accepted the prevailing feminist dogma that ignores the roles God assigned us and the biological realities of gender differences. Most Protestant church leaders today have decided that the timeless authority of Scripture should be subordinated to a dysfunctional system of gender values that is only a few decades old.

The success of the feminism psyop serves as indisputable proof that women are more easily deceived than men. Just as Satan targeted Eve in the Garden of Eden, the social engineers who turned the sexes against each other did so by targeting women and convincing them that they were being victimized. They understood that the female gender was the more vulnerable target, so that is where they concentrated their efforts. The social engineers also knew that women's innate solipsism would blind them to the catastrophic consequences that feminism would have for society as a whole.

What do you suppose would have happened if the social engineers had targeted men with their brainwashing campaign? Despite the fact that men in the West have at least as many grievances as women do, most men would have simply ignored the suggestion that the opposite sex was somehow responsible for victimizing them. The psyop would have failed.

Another proof that women are more easily deceived than men is their propensity for pursuing witchcraft. This practice has always attracted a predominantly female following. Records of the witch trials that took place in Europe between the 15th and 18th centuries show that between 80 and 85 per cent of witches were female.[2]

"GIVE NOT THY STRENGTH UNTO WOMEN, NOR THY WAYS TO THAT WHICH DESTROYETH KINGS." - PROVERBS 31:3

There has been a dramatic increase in the number of witches and practitioners of Wicca in the past few decades. In the U.S., the number skyrocketed from 8,000 in 1990 to 1.5 million today.[3] This increase is tied to feminist propaganda that pushes witchcraft as a form of female empowerment. It's especially attractive to the young and naive. Teenage girls are drawn to it because it's trendy and they get to wear stylish gothic clothes and ornate silver jewellery. They eagerly await the day when they will be able to put hexes on the boys who dumped them. Few understand that they're creating a connection with Satan when they go down this road.

Given the plain facts of female solipsism and vulnerability to deception, any church with the slightest interest in its own self preservation would mandate an exclusively male clergy. Let's look at a few case studies to see what happens when this simple safeguard isn't observed.

Margaret Ann "Gretta" Vosper (1958-) is a pastor with the United Church of Canada (Canada's largest Protestant denomination). Not having anything meaningful to say about Scripture, she decided to talk about herself instead, and declared in 2013 that she is an atheist. This bizarre admission launched five years of debate in the church about whether or not she should be allowed to remain a pastor. The insanity of this chain of events was topped only by the outcome: at the end of the five year period, it was decided that she could keep her job.[4]

This shameful slice of church history encapsulates everything that is wrong with Protestantism today. The United Church of Canada can no longer be called a church, and anyone who continues to remain a member does not understand what it means to be a Christian, let alone a Protestant.

A legitimate church would immediately eject any pastor who called the existence of God into question. By allowing someone who openly defies doctrine to continue preaching, the church negates itself. Rather than bringing people closer to God, it is doing the opposite. The United Church is thus best described not as a church, which is an organization of Christians, but as an anti-church.

Unlike Catholicism, Protestantism has no centralized authority overseeing its member churches. Each denomination is a discrete entity. This is one instance where the Catholic model has an advantage. Although Catholic churches may disagree on the finer points of doctrine, they have thus far managed to keep female priests from becoming commonplace. Of course, Pope Francis is doing all he can to promote his own brand of dysfunction, which includes unconditional support for gay rights. In 2023, the pope fired American bishop Joseph Strickland for criticizing his LGBTQ agenda.[5]

The second case study we'll cover is Eva Brunne, the world's first lesbian bishop. She served as the Bishop of Stockholm from 2009 to 2019. Brunne's infamous contribution to the Church of Sweden (Sweden's Evangelical Lutheran Church) was her recommendation to remove all crosses from the Seamen's Mission Church in Stockholm and install a Muslim prayer space in 2015.[6]

Brunne's dimwitted suggestion to desecrate a Protestant church was but one manifestation of the pathological altruism that gripped Sweden when the European migrant crisis began in 2015. Predominantly Muslim migrants from Syria, North Africa and the Middle East were given the red carpet treatment when they arrived in Sweden in vast numbers. The Swedes were so invested in virtue signalling that their feminist government unwittingly orchestrated the nation's suicide by welcoming these migrants and showering them with generous incentives.

The migrants took Sweden's government by surprise when they not only failed to assimilate, but turned the formerly peaceful and relatively crime free country into the rape capital of Europe. Only today are a few Swedish politicians beginning to step forward and admit that their great immigration experiment was a dismal failure.

Violent crime has skyrocketed since 2015 and Swedish citizens can no longer walk the streets in safety. There are numerous no-go zones throughout the country where police and ambulance services cannot operate because they're ambushed by violent mobs. Bombings in urban areas, which were unheard of a few years ago, are now commonplace. The country may never fully recover from its tragic misstep.[7]

As political sentiment in Sweden slowly begins to turn against migration, some may remember the misguided antics of Eva Brunne, but it is doubtful that she will ever atone for her stupidity. What is worse is that her admittance to the office of bishop has forever sullied what was formerly an esteemed and respected position in the church. All those who subsequently serve as Bishop of Stockholm will simply be filling the shoes of a clown.

In the Church of England, The Ven Miranda Threlfall-Holmes, Archdeacon of Liverpool, seems to feel that her office is a platform from which to share her mental health issues with everyone. She said the following on X (formerly Twitter):

I went to a conference on whiteness last autumn. It was very good, very interesting and made me realise: whiteness is to race as patriarchy is to gender. So yes, let's have anti whiteness, & let's smash the patriarchy.[8]

Former UKIP leader Nigel Farage responded to this blatantly misandrist and racist post by lambasting Church of England leaders as hopeless. He observed that these leaders have surrendered to the woke agenda and described Threlfall-Holmes as "out of touch with reality."[9] He didn't mention that she is white, which makes her comment even more bizarre.

Threlfall-Holmes, like most middle-aged feminists who have strayed into a job for which they're not qualified, is doing something far worse than being a bigot. She is worshipping false idols and leveraging her position to spread this false worship to anyone who will listen. For the Church of England to tolerate this behaviour from any member of its clergy is a clear indicator that it has fully apostatized.

The clown ladies we've covered in this chapter are not isolated cases. They reflect the solipsism and vulnerability to deception that are endemic to female clergy. These individuals are not leaders, but overgrown children who gloat over the immunity they've been given from taking responsibility for their actions. They mock Christianity and disgrace their churches.

The term 'female clergy' should be regarded as an oxymoron. Any church treating the term otherwise is guaranteed to fail.

1. "Americans Prefer Male Boss to a Female Boss." https://news.gallup.com/poll/24346/americans-prefer-male-boss-female-boss.aspx
2. Pócs, Éva. "Why Witches are Women." Acta Ethnographic Hungarica, 2003. pp. 367-383. *https://www.researchgate.net/publication/250007762_Why_Witches_Are_Women*
3. Fearnow, Benjamin. "Number Of Witches Rises Dramatically Across U.S. As Millennials Reject Christianity." Newsweek, November 18, 2018. https://www.newsweek.com/witchcraft-wiccans-mysticism-astrology-witches-millennials-pagans-religion-1221019
4. Longhurst, John. "Atheist minister Gretta Vosper hopes to stay at Canadian church for the long haul." Religion News Service, February 1, 2019. https://religionnews.com/2019/02/01/atheist-minister-gretta-vosper-hopes-to-stay-at-canadian-church-for-the-long-haul/
5. "Pope fires anti-LGBTQ bishop." RT. https://www.rt.com/news/587094-pope-francis-fires-critic-bishop/
6. Lane, Oliver. "World's first lesbian bishop calls for church to remove crosses, to install Muslim prayer space." Breitbart, October 5, 2015. https://www.breitbart.com/europe/2015/10/05/worlds-first-lesbian-bishop-calls-church-remove-crosses-install-muslim-prayer-space/
7. Wilson, Bob. *The Big Fake: How Killing the Sexes is Killing the West.* Self-published, 2021, p. 104.
8. "Church of England archdeacon calls for 'anti-whiteness' and 'smashing the patriarchy' but insists she is not 'anti-white' or 'anti-men'." Mail Online. https://www.dailymail.co.uk/news/article-13234375/Church-England-archdeacon-anti-whiteness-smashing-patriarchy.html
9. "Nigel Farage reveals he's 'given up' on attending church because CofE bosses have 'surrendered' to a 'woke agenda' as he slams archdeacon's call for 'anti-whiteness'." CitiGist. https://citigist.com/news/nigel-farage-reveals-hes-given-up-on-attending-church-because-cofe-bosses-have-surrendered-to-a-woke-agenda-as-he-slams-archdeacons-call-for-anti-whiteness/

ΑΩ
THE ECUMENICAL MOVEMENT

Ecumenism is the idea that those of various faiths should put aside their differences and come together to form one big happy family. It sounds great on the surface. After all, there is strength in numbers.

The problem with ecumenism is that it requires compromise. Although compromise works in many organizational settings, it doesn't always work when doctrine is involved. To take an example, if Seventh-day Adventists were to merge with any other Protestant denomination, they would have to accept Sunday worship. In so doing, they would be erasing their identity as Seventh-day Adventists.

Despite the limitations of ecumenism, some early successes were achieved in the Protestant realm. The appropriately named United Church of Canada was founded in 1925 as a merger of the Methodist Church, the Congregational Union of Ontario and Quebec, two-thirds of the congregations of the Presbyterian Church in Canada, and various smaller churches in the Prairies.[1]

The formation of the United Church a century ago demonstrates that when differences in doctrine are minor, denominational mergers can work. However, the ecumenical movement has taken a startling turn over the last several decades. This movement aims to merge not only Christian denominations, but all the world's religions, with all their vastly different belief systems, into one. The key players behind the contemporary ecumenical movement include the Roman Catholic Church (RCC) and the Jesuit Order, the CIA, and the Rockefeller family.

In his video "Angels, Demons & Intelligence Agencies," geopolitical analyst Jay Dyer discusses the close ties between U.S. alphabet agencies and the Vatican. He references Michael Graziano's book *Errand into the Wilderness of Mirrors: Religion and the History of the CIA*, explaining that these agencies have an interest in religion as a tool to control public opinion. He also discusses the relationship between the Jesuit Order and the CIA, noting that the CIA has strong connections with leading Jesuit colleges in the U.S.

The Vatican alliance with American intelligence agencies dates back to the Cold War. Dyer posits that the CIA has endeavoured for more than half a century to leverage the power of the Vatican to promote ecumenism on a worldwide scale. The end goal that these agencies hope to achieve is the total subversion of organized Christianity.[2]

The Second Vatican Council, which took place from 1962 to 1965, was a milestone in the ecumenical movement. The core theme of the council was reconciliation with other faiths—both Christian and non-Christian. On the surface, this looked like a noble effort to unite various religions under one banner. However, there were two key objectives that were not publicized as part of the official agenda.

The first hidden objective of the council was to install the RCC as the de facto leader of the new one world religion that would eventually emerge. The second was to remove the KJV Bible once and for all from organized Christianity.

With the RCC as head of the new one world religion, it would have the power to unilaterally decide which version of the Bible to use. In fact, the RCC would be in a position to create an entirely new Bible to take into account the disparate views of the various faiths assembling under its umbrella. The KJV Bible—the definitive version of Scripture that has been a thorn in the side of the RCC for half a millennium—would finally be eliminated.

Over the past decade or so, Pope Francis has continued to promote increased cooperation between various religious organizations, even extending an invitation to the Islamic faith. In 2019, the joint declaration "A Document on Human Fraternity for World Peace and Living Together" was signed by Pope Francis and Sheikh Ahmad el-Tayeb, a grand imam of Sunni Muslims, during a visit by the pope to the United Arab Emirates.[3] This document was adopted by world religious leaders at the 7th World Religions Congress in September 2022.

This event has been described as the codification and ratification of 'Chrislam,' an ill-advised attempt at merging Christianity and Islam. Highlights of the document include the following:

We note that pluralism in terms of differences in skin color, gender, race, language and culture are expressions of the wisdom of God in creation. Religious diversity is permitted by God and, therefore, any coercion to a particular religion and religious doctrine is unacceptable.

We recognize the importance and value of the Document on Human Fraternity for World Peace and

Living Together between the Holy See and Al-Azhar Al-Sharif (adopted by the UN General Assembly in resolution A/RES/75/200 of December 21, 2020), and the Makkah Declaration (adopted in Mecca in May 2019), which call for peace, dialogue, mutual understanding and mutual respect among believers for the common good.

We call upon religious leaders and prominent political figures from different parts of the world tirelessly to develop dialogue in the name of friendship, solidarity and peaceful coexistence.

We appeal to all people of faith and goodwill to unite in this difficult time and contribute to ensuring security and harmony in our common home – planet Earth.[4]

These talking points seem well-intentioned at first glance, but a thorough reading of the document reveals that nowhere is any mention made of Jesus Christ. This is the smoking gun, revealing that 'Chrislam' is not actually a merger of two religions, but the subjugation of Christianity under a false doctrine.

The new universal religion being created by the Vatican is a prerequisite for the New World Order. The technocrats are well aware of the fact that Christianity, as expressed in the Protestant tenet of Sola Scriptura, is the last great barrier to implementing the New World Order. That is why the Vatican and its partner, the CIA, have been tasked with subverting it.

The New World Order has been advertised by U.S. presidents and other political leaders for many years, and it seems to be on the cusp of coming to fruition. It's the soon to be realized vision of a world in which we'll own nothing and be happy, as the ads tell us. It's a global empire envisioned by the World Economic Forum (WEF) to operate under a technocratic framework. In other words, the world will be ordered according to the dictates of science.

This sounds like a rational approach. After all, we can trust in science, can't we?

The Covid-19 scamdemic of 2020 told us all we need to know about the trustworthiness of science. This carefully planned psyop was a test run for the launch of the New World Order. The WEF website states: "The pandemic represents a rare but narrow window of opportunity to reflect, reimagine, and reset our world."[5]

Let's review what science and its government supporters told us during and after the scamdemic:

- ▸ We just need two weeks to flatten the curve
- ▸ Masks are not effective, but we must wear them anyway
- ▸ Covid tests produce false results, but we must take them anyway and abide by the results
- ▸ Vaccines are safe and effective, but may cause myocarditis, Bells Palsy, immune system disorders, cancer, and a host of other side effects, including sudden death

In retrospect, the science was wrong. How could it be that it let us down when we needed it the most? After all, scientists have a reputation for being honest, forthright individuals. Their public image is as pristine as their white lab coats. We want to believe that they work tirelessly and selflessly for the betterment of mankind.

"BEWARE OF FALSE PROPHETS, WHICH COME TO YOU IN SHEEP'S CLOTHING, BUT INWARDLY THEY ARE RAVENING WOLVES." - MATTHEW 7:15

The reality is that like most people, scientists earn salaries by working for an employer. These employers are beholden to company shareholders to generate a profit. If a scientist makes a discovery that won't generate sufficient revenue, it's tagged as unprofitable and discarded. Whether or not this discovery is beneficial to the rest of us is irrelevant. The scientist is instructed to abandon the finding and move on to the next project.

In some cases, it's even worse, and the scientist is told to falsify their findings to bring them in line with corporate objectives. A former colleague of mine who worked in the research industry told me an interesting story about the assignment he had while on his work term in graduate school. Upon sharing the bad news about a promising hypothesis that unfortunately wasn't proven by the results of the research, he was given the following choice: continue the research and find a positive way to interpret the findings to support the continuation of the project, or receive no further funding.

Some scientists—those with a conscience—persist in pursuing discoveries that go against the company mandate because of the potential benefit to mankind. These individuals all meet the same fate: they're given fifteen minutes to put their belongings in a box and vacate the company premises. They also tend to encounter difficulties when attempting to seek future employment, and may find themselves slandered and disowned by the scientific community. In some cases, they may become victims of a fatal accident, purely by coincidence of course.

Knowing that science is controlled by profit driven companies, the next question to ask is, who controls the companies? Companies are subject to the corporate laws that govern the country in which they operate. As long as they don't get caught laundering money or committing some other crime, they're free to do as they please. However, when looking at all the companies that have jumped on the woke bandwagon in recent years, it quickly becomes evident that there's more going on than meets the eye.

The term fascism conjures up images of men with small moustaches and megalomaniacal tendencies commanding hordes of jackbooted soldiers. For the true meaning of the word, we turn to former dictator of Italy Benito Mussolini (1883-1945). The following quote is attributed to Mussolini: "Fascism should more properly be called corporatism because it is the merger of state and corporate power."[6]

By this definition, fascism is present in most modern political systems, including communism and capitalism alike. What is occurring in the West today is the global implementation of fascism as a precursor to a technocratic New World Order. Companies like Budweiser and Disney didn't go woke out of a suicidal urge to kill their profits, but because they were compelled to. So deeply are they enmeshed in the fascist system that they sacrificed profits in order to support the narrative mandated by their handlers.

Just as corporate activity must be coralled under a centralized globalist authority in order to bring the New World Order into being, so too must religion be controlled. This is why a one world religion is on the agenda. This religion will be anti-Christian—a Frankenstein's monster of doctrines from different faiths, headed by the pope and the RCC.

If the WEF's agenda doesn't convince you that the New World Order is just around the corner, all you need do is consult Revelation. It is prophesied in precise detail.

1. "United Church of Canada." Britannica. https://www.britannica.com/topic/United-Church-of-Canada
2. "Angels, Demons & Intelligence Agencies." Odysee. https://odysee.com/@JayDyer:8/angels,-demons-intelligence-agencies-jay:3
3. Doyle, Kenneth. One world religion. The Pilot, March 20, 2019, https://www.thebostonpilot.com/article.php?ID=184609
4. Grider, Geoffrey. Chrislam confirmed. Now the End Begins, Sept. 17, 2022. https://www.nowtheendbegins.com/7th-congress-of-leaders-of-world-religions-adopt-human-fraternity-chrislam-document-pope-francis-mohamed-bin-zayed/
5. Schwab, Klaus. The Great Reset. https://www.weforum.org/focus/the-great-reset
6. Berlet, Chip. "Mussolini on the Corporate State." Political Research Associates, January 12, 2005. https://politicalresearch.org/2005/01/12/mussolini-corporate-state

AΩ
NEW AGE CHURCHES

The New Age movement is synonymous with modern, progressive thinking. Its origins can be traced back to the beginning of the 20th century. French Jesuit priest Pierre Teilhard de Chardin (1881-1955) was one of the earliest proponents of New Age thought, and is often mentioned as a key source of inspiration by New Age advocates. He advocated for autotheism and pantheism, which we'll explore in detail in this chapter. Some of his famous quotes include "I can be saved only by becoming one with the universe" and "Each one of us is evolving towards the God-head."[1]

New Age thought experienced a boom during the counterculture movement of the 1960s and was further cultivated by theosophist David Spangler in the 1970s. Encyclopedia Britannica says the following about Spangler:

> In 1970 American theosophist David Spangler moved to the Findhorn Foundation, where he developed the fundamental idea of the New Age movement. He believed that the release of new waves of spiritual energy, signaled by certain astrological changes (e.g., the movement of the Earth into a new cycle known as the Age of Aquarius), had initiated the coming of the New Age. He further suggested that people use this new energy to make manifest the New Age. . .

Returning to the United States in the mid-1970s, Spangler became the major architect of the movement. He presented his ideas in a set of popular books beginning with *Revelation: The Birth of a New Age* (1976) and attracted many leaders from older occult and metaphysical organizations to the growing movement.[2]

The New Age movement is still immensely popular today. It is based on the following beliefs:

▶ No absolutes (truth and morality are relative and personal)
▶ Autotheism (we can become gods)
▶ Pluralism (all paths lead to God)
▶ The law of attraction (like attracts like)
▶ Pantheism (the Creator and Creation are one)[3]

Anyone with a passing knowledge of Scripture will immediately discern that all five of these beliefs are incompatible with a Christian worldview. Nevertheless, New Age thinking has resulted in the growth of a type of faux Protestantism known as Charismatic Christianity. Charismatic churches stress the importance of miracles and supernatural events in the day to day lives of their followers. These churches draw on New Age concepts to concoct a belief system that incorporates elements of Buddhism, Hinduism, and Satanism. Let's look at each of these five New Age beliefs in detail.

The idea that there are no absolutes when it comes to truth and morality directly contravenes Christian doctrine. Relative morality is a contradiction in terms. For morality to have any meaning, it must be universal. Man cannot decide what is moral or immoral because human beings are inconstant and flawed. A simple proof of this is to ask several people if abortion is right or wrong. Some will answer in the affirmative and some in the negative. No amount of debate will settle the matter. For universal morality to exist, it must be defined by God.

Many atheists argue that they don't need religion to live a morally just life. They say that they would never kill another human being because it's simply wrong, and they don't need the Bible to tell them that. What they don't realize is that their innate sense of morality was bestowed upon them by the environment in which they grew up. Most people living in the West have been exposed to Christian morality. They have developed a Christian sense of what is right and wrong whether they realize it or not. In short, many atheists are closet Christians, and they don't know it.

Suggesting that truth is relative leads to even greater issues. Science requires absolute truth. It is only through God that we're given constant physical laws that create uniformity in nature. In his book *The Ultimate Proof of Creation*, Jason Lisle states:

> The biblical creationist expects there to be order in the universe because God made all things (Gen. 1:1; John 1:3) and has imposed order on the universe.[4]

Knowing that these laws can be counted on to be in effect tomorrow as they were today is essential to making scientific predictions. Without the absolute truths defined by God, there can be no science. We would be doomed to eternal ignorance, stumbling in the dark until the end of days.

Autotheism is a particularly seductive concept. When the science fiction film *Star Wars Episode IV: A New Hope* premiered in 1977, it revived interest in spiritualism. Borrowing from concepts found in Eastern spirituality, director George Lucas came up with the idea of The Force, a universal energy that could be harnessed by someone trained in the Jedi arts. By learning to control this reservoir of hidden energy, Jedi Knights could levitate objects, bend the will of the weak minded, and even hurl energy bolts. In short, they were demigods.

The notion of the heroic Jedi Knight with superhuman powers was calculated to thrill the imaginations of young moviegoers, and it succeeded brilliantly. It all seemed like harmless fun at the time.

Taking a step back and re-evaluating *Star Wars* from a biblical standpoint, the concept of the Jedi Knight leans dangerously close to autotheism. The only way that a human being could develop Jedi-like powers would be by selling their soul to Satan. There have been rare occasions when God granted superhuman powers to His children, as when He gave Moses the power to turn a wooden staff into a snake or part the Red Sea. However, in each case, these powers were granted only temporarily through God's grace.

There has been a resurgence of superhero films in recent decades, including *Superman* (dir. Richard Donner, 1978) and its sequels, *Spiderman* (dir. Sam Raimi, 2002) and its sequels, and the long-lived *X-Men* franchise that started in 2000. All these films promote autotheism by featuring characters with superhuman powers.

What is especially pernicious about the *X-Men* films is that they cast ordinary human beings as villains. The subtext is that being ordinary is equivalent to being evil. This is a subtle form of brainwashing intended to groom people for the transhumanist agenda, in which people become technologically enhanced quasi-robots. The implied promise is that if you go along with this agenda, you too can be superhuman. The recent rise in popularity of body modification—promoted by pop stars and media personalities—is a precursor to transhumanism. Tattoos and piercings are intended to normalize the act of modifying your body. Someone who already has several piercings won't think twice about getting a subcutaneous RFID chip or other electronic implant.

The New Age ideal of pluralism posits that all religions and systems of faith are acceptable. This is a precondition for the one world religion agenda currently being pushed by the Vatican. A one world religion requires that Jesus Christ be de-emphasized or eliminated. It is tantamount to the destruction of Christianity.

"REGARD NOT THEM THAT HAVE FAMILIAR SPIRITS, NEITHER SEEK AFTER WIZARDS, TO BE DEFILED BY THEM: I AM THE LORD YOUR GOD." - LEVITICUS 19:31

The World Economic Forum (WEF) assures us that in the coming New World Order, we will own nothing and be happy. It will be similar to the society described by Aldous Huxley in his science fiction novel *Brave New World*. The WEF recognizes that Christianity is the greatest threat to the New World Order, and this is why the Vatican has been assigned to replace it with a one world religion that denies Christ.

If you believe that the WEF is a harmless think tank with no jurisdiction over individual nations, understand that most political leaders in the West today are WEF puppets. They've been installed in positions of power for a reason. The globally coordinated response to the Covid-19 scamdemic of 2020 demonstrated that the nations of the world will bow down to a centralized global authority without question when so instructed.

The law of attraction is another seemingly well intentioned New Age concept, and was popularized in the bestselling book *The Secret* by Rhonda Bryne. It is defined thus:

> The law of attraction is a philosophy suggesting that positive thoughts bring positive results into a person's life, while negative thoughts bring negative outcomes. It is based on the belief that thoughts are a form of energy and that positive energy attracts success in all areas of life, including health, finances, and relationships.[5]

The idea that you can achieve your goals by positive visualization harkens back to The Force in *Star Wars*. It is essentially The Force Lite and is a form of autotheism because it suggests that human beings have superhuman powers. We know from Scripture that such powers are not available to us.

The term 'The Law of Attraction' was in fact coined by Luciferian occultist Helena Blavatsky in the late 1800s.[6] Blavatsky cofounded the Theosophical Society in the U.S. in 1875. Its members were obsessed with Gnosticism and Satanism. The theosophical movement became a springboard for the spread of occultism in the early 1900s, particularly among the wealthier classes in the U.S. As Christianity fell out of favour, many political and financial leaders began taking an interest in the occult.[7]

Pantheism, which is the Hinduist/Buddhist idea that we are one with nature, and that this unity is divine, is clearly anti-Christian. Scripture tells us that God created everything, including us, and that we are separate from God. Moreover, we are not divine. Although God is

178

omniscient and omnipresent, he does not permeate nature in the way described in Eastern religions.

It's easy to see how the Charismatic movement established a foothold. From a branding perspective, this type of church enjoys a unique competitive advantage over traditional churches. By championing New Age concepts, the potential customer base is widened to attract those who are lukewarm about Christianity but get excited about healing crystals.

One such church is Bethel Church in the U.S. state of California. A marketer's dream, it employs not only New Age thinking to attract followers, but also owns Bethel Music, a Christian music label and artist collective. Bethel Church even has its own New Testament and translation of Psalms, known as *The Passion Translation*. Translator Brian Simmons has been severely criticized for the liberties he took with this work. Theological journal Themelios has the following to say about *The Passion Translation*:

> Brian Simmons has made a new translation of the Psalms (and now the whole New Testament) which aims to 're-introduce the passion and fire of the Bible to the English reader.' He achieves this by abandoning all interest in textual accuracy, playing fast and loose with the original languages, and inserting so much new material into the text that it is at least 50% longer than the original. The result is a strongly sectarian translation that no longer counts as Scripture; by masquerading as a Bible it threatens to bind entire churches in thrall to a false god.[8]

Pastors who preach New Age concepts are doing a disservice to Protestantism. Scratch the surface and it quickly becomes evident that the entire New Age movement has its roots in occultism and is completely at odds with Scripture. It has no place in the Protestant Church.

1. Veith, Walter J. "Teilhard's Spirituality." Amazing Dicoveries. https://amazingdiscoveries.org/S-deception_UN-Teilhard_Maitreya_Omega
2. "New Age Movement." Britannica. https://www.britannica.com/topic/New-Age-movement
3. "The New Age Movement has Infiltrated the Church." The Set-Apart Walk. November 25, 2022. https://thesetapartwalk.com/the-new-age-movement-has-infiltrated-the-church/
4. Lisle, Dr. Jason. *The Ultimate Proof of Creation.* Master Books, 2009, p.62.
5. Scott, Elizabeth. "What is the Law of Attraction?" VeryWellMind, November 7, 2022. https://www.verywellmind.com/understanding-and-using-the-law-of-attraction-3144808
6. Bancarz, Steven. "The Law Of Attraction Explained & Debunked." Reasons for Jesus, February 4, 2020. https://reasonsforjesus.com/the-law-of-attraction-explained-debunked/
7. Smith, Brandon. "To Understand The Globalists We Must Understand Their Psychopathic Religion." Alt-Market. https://alt-market.us/to-understand-the-globalists-we-must-understand-their-psychopathic-religion/
8. Shead, Andrew. "Burning Scripture with Passion: A Review of The Psalms (The Passion Translation)." Themelios. https://www.thegospelcoalition.org/themelios/article/burning-scripture-with-passion-a-review-of-the-psalms-passion-translation/

ΑΩ
ONE GOOD PASTOR

After meeting some of the characters in the preceding chapters, you might be wondering if there are any good pastors left. I don't want to create the impression that all pastors should be regarded with suspicion, so I'll end this section on a positive note.

There are still a few good pastors doing God's work. An excellent example is Pastor Artur Pawlowski of Calgary, Canada. In 2005, he began a street church service to feed the homeless in Calgary. He was arrested and charged in 2006 for reading the Bible in public. Yes, in the post-Christian country of Canada, it is illegal to read the Bible in public. Between 2005 and 2015, Pawlowski received over 300 citations for preaching and feeding the homeless.[1]

"THOUGH HE FALL, HE SHALL NOT BE UTTERLY CAST DOWN: FOR THE LORD UPHOLDETH HIM WITH HIS HAND." - PSALM 37:24

For his charitable works, he has not only been imprisoned, but has been held in solitary confinement, tortured, and denied access to his lawyer. While he was in prison, he was given two Bibles, both of which were confiscated.

Pawlowski was an ardent defender of human rights during the Covid-19 scamdemic, standing up to authorities and defying the draconian restrictions placed on Canadians' freedoms. For his sermons to the truckers who staged a peaceful protest in 2022 against Covid restrictions in Canada, Pawlowski now faces up to ten years in prison.[2]

Pastor Artur Pawlowski's charitable works and brave stand against tyranny are an inspiration to all. Ironically, it's doubtful that his name will ever be mentioned in any seminary, since these institutions are more concerned with being politically correct than with championing someone who goes against the system. Nevertheless, the Protestant Church would benefit from having more pastors like Artur Pawlowksi.

1. Durden, Tyler. "Canadian Pastor Convicted Of Inciting Mischief In Trucker Protests Facing Up To 10 Years Prison." Zerohedge, August 1, 2023. https://www.zerohedge.com/political/canadian-pastor-convicted-inciting-mischief-trucker-protests-facing-10-years-prison
2. Ibid.

AΩ

QUESTIONS TO ASK BEFORE JOINING A CHURCH

When shopping for martial arts classes, it's customary for the chief instructor of a school to invite you to a free introductory class. This gives you the opportunity to meet the instructor and see how you get along, ask each other about your respective martial arts backgrounds, and determine if the school will be a good fit for your training goals. You might try two or three schools before making your selection.

Choosing a church, which is a considerably more important decision, is rarely done with this level of diligence. Most people will attend a service before joining, but few would think of arranging to meet with the pastor before deciding.

Request a meeting if you have the opportunity. If the pastor declines, consider this a red flag. A pastor who is unwilling to speak with potential new members about joining may prove to be similarly unhelpful in providing you the spiritual guidance you're looking for after you join.

If the pastor agrees to meet, have some questions prepared beforehand. Depending on how much time you have, you may not be able to get all the answers you want, so choose your questions carefully. You may be able to get some of the answers to more general questions by speaking to members of the congregation.

When meeting with the pastor, pay attention to how clear and direct the answers are. Do you get a sense of conviction, or does he seem to be hedging? Consider what your gut tells you in addition to the raw content of the answers. The pastor may string the right words together, but if you don't trust what you're hearing, or feel that something is off, it may be a sign that you need to keep looking.

Here are some questions you might wish to ask the pastor to get you started (naturally you'll want to add your own questions as well):

► Which version of the Bible does the church use?
► Do you believe that Christian and secular worldviews are compatible?
► Do you believe in creation or evolution?
► What do you think of Sola Scriptura?
► Who or what is the antichrist?
► What is the mark of the beast?
► What are your views on Martin Luther?
► Should Protestants reconcile with the Catholic Church?
► How do you feel about a one world religion?
► Is the Israel of the Old Testament the same as the Israel of today?
► Do you believe in a pre-tribulation rapture?

I've met pastors who have said all kinds of surprising things. Some have claimed that certain books of the New Testament are more valid than others, while others have remarked that the Bible shouldn't be taken too literally because it was written a long time ago. You can run into a vast range of opinions, so it's worth doing a little preliminary research to avoid surprises later.

"HE THAT WALKETH WITH WISE MEN SHALL BE WISE: BUT A COMPANION OF FOOLS SHALL BE DESTROYED." - PROVERBS 13:20

Pastors are vulnerable to the same social conditioning that is foisted on all of us. One of the most harmful psyops currently in play is feminism. Decades of brainwashing has infected a lot of minds with harmful nonsense about gender roles.

If your pastor doesn't understand that feminism was introduced to to destroy the family, reduce the birthrate, give control of children to the state, and get the entire population to pay income tax, then you're better off looking for another church.

Christianity is based on a hierarchical family structure that's only workable when traditional gender roles are respected. This means the husband is the leader of the household. The husband obeys God, the wife obeys the husband, and the children obey the parents.

By the same token, a pastor who blindly accepts mainstream narratives about climate change, 9/11 and the like will not enhance your personal growth as a Christian. There's little point listening to sermons that echo the fabricated agendas of the mainstream media. This type of pastor will not bring you closer to God, but will separate you from Him.

If you visited several churches, interviewed their pastors, and didn't find what you were looking for, there's no need to despair. In the next chapter, we'll look at an alternative to joining a church that can be at least as

effective, if not more so, in helping you build a relationship
with God.

ΑΩ
THE ALTERNATIVE TO JOINING A CHURCH

In the preceding chapters, we covered the reasons people like to attend church, explored the role of the pastor, and looked at the impact of secular developments like feminism and affirmative action on the Protestant Church. We also looked at the relatively recent phenomenon of New Age churches.

We discussed how the foundational Protestant precept of Sola Scriptura is rarely heeded in most Protestant churches today, and how the Word of God is filtered through a modern day secular perspective. We talked about pastors who parrot the Current Thing and are worried about being politically correct.

Faced with the broken state of organized Protestantism today, you might be wondering how you'll ever find a church that will help bring you closer to God. The answer is that you don't have to. Protestantism has always stressed the importance of cutting out the middleman and forging a direct relationship with God. Luther called out the RCC for turning faith into a complicated bureaucratic process that was neither biblical nor beneficial. If we follow this philosophy to its logical conclusion, it becomes clear that attending church is unnecessary.

Many of the greatest figures in the Bible earned their place in history by following God on their own, without the help of a community. Noah had no church to go to in the days before the Flood. In fact, he was surrounded by corruption: "The earth also was corrupt before God, and the earth was filled with violence" (Genesis 6:11).

Imagine what an atheist would have thought when observing Noah building a massive ship in the middle of a field. He might have advised him that there would be no way to transport the ship to the nearest lake or river once it was finished. Had Noah told the man that torrential rains would soon flood the earth, he would have been met with disbelief.

Noah built a relationship with God that was as unshakeable as any human being could hope for, and he cultivated this relationship without the support of a church. Noah had faith in God, was obedient to Him, and stood alone with Him.[1]

"THOU ART NOT FAR FROM THE KINGDOM OF GOD." - MARK 12:34

When you stand alone with God, you achieve a connection far stronger than would be possible via the conduit of a church. In a congregation, it's easy for someone unsure of their faith to sit in the back row and use the church as a buffer while they overcome their doubts. Noah did not have this luxury. His faith had to be completely pure for him to succeed at the epic task that was handed to him.

Studying the Bible without the support of a congregation is easier than ever thanks to the plentiful online resources available. Audiobooks of the Old and New Testaments that provide text with narration allow content to more readily absorbed because you're processing audio and video simultaneously. I find that an audiobook sinks in much better than opening a hardcopy KJV Bible and wading through it on my own.

Once you've familiarized yourself with the text of the Bible, there's no end to the amount of time you can spend researching summaries, analyses, and discussions of anything and everything related to Scripture. You have an unlimited source of information to draw on, with a diversity of viewpoints that no single congregation could ever offer. Why limit yourself to the voice of a single pastor at a bricks and mortar church when you can select from the best of hundreds of online sources?

The biggest challenge is finding good quality content, since much of what passes for Christian content on YouTube, Odysee, Bitchute, Rumble, Rokfin, and other video platforms is in fact blatantly anti-Christian. Another challenge is getting around the increasingly aggressive censorship that keeps viewers from discovering good Christian content. YouTube, which is still the most popular video platform, is also the most notorious for censorship.

Large web hosting providers like Wordpress are also vehemently anti-Christian. One site with Christian content, www.hugotalks.com, had its subscriber mailings blocked by Wordpress.

The better the quality of the videos, the more censorship a content provider encounters. If you see a vlogger get kicked off YouTube, it's often a sign that they have solid content. Getting banned from YouTube is a feather in the cap for the vlogger who values truth over political correctness. Keep track of your favourite vloggers when they migrate to Bitchute, Odysee, Rumble or Brighteon.

Depending on where you live, using a VPN can increase your pool of available content by eliminating regional restrictions. Using a good search engine is also important. If you're still using Google, you're preventing yourself from accessing a vast pool of content that has been buried by algorithms or deleted outright. The Internet you see through Google gets smaller every day, since any content that doesn't support the Current Thing is being methodically eliminated. Alternatives like Entireweb, Qwant and Yandex are somewhat better.

Authentic Protestant content is increasingly being driven underground. It's my hope that the underground web will continue to provide a safe haven for Christian content providers who are banned from mainstream platforms. Just in the last decade or so, finding this type of content has become far more difficult. It's still there, but you have to put in the effort to find it.

The fact that you're reading this book indicates that you enjoy traditional media as well, and books have become an underutilized resource. One of the benefits of a hardcopy book is that once it's in your possession, no-one can censor it. It also goes without saying that not every book that's in hardcopy can be found online. I have several books in my library that are either not available online, or are only available in censored versions.

You might be wondering if watching sermons on television is a viable alternative to going to church in person. What you see on television is called programming for a reason. It programs you to think a certain way.

Television throughout the West is controlled by the global mainstream media cartel. The only content that makes it onto television is that which supports the Current Thing. In a preceding chapter, we covered the rise and fall of televangelist Billy Graham, a freemason who represents everything that is wrong with televised church services. Protestant pastors you see on television—at least the ones delivering services in English—are probably compromised in the same way that Graham was.

Televangelist Kenneth Copeland, considered the wealthiest pastor in the U.S., has an estimated net worth of $760 million. He lives in a $7 million mansion tax free, thanks to a loophole that allows him to claim his home as a clergy residence. When recently asked to account for his lavish lifestyle, Copeland sideskirted the question and said, "It takes a lot of money to do what we do. We have brought over 122 million people to the Lord Jesus Christ."[2]

At the beginning of this chapter I cited Noah as an inspiration to Protestants. The disastrous state of most churches today makes an outcast of those of us who wish to honour Martin Luther's tenet of Sola Scriptura and follow the Word of God. In a sense, we're in a similar position to Noah.

We can learn a great deal from Noah's perseverance. His faith was strong, and he was not deterred by the prospect of going it alone. He succeeded in completing the monumental task set before him without the support of friends or neighbours. Noah had no church. However, he made the decision to obey God, and the rewards he reaped speak for themselves.

1. "Lesson 11: The Men Who Had Connections With God (Ezekiel 14:12-20)." Bible.org. https://bible.org/seriespage/lesson-11-men-who-had-connections-god-ezekiel-1412-20

2. "Kenneth Copeland, wealthiest US pastor, lives on $7M tax-free estate." New York Post, December 17, 2021. https://nypost.com/2021/12/17/kenneth-copeland-wealthiest-us-pastor-lives-on-7m-tax-free-estate/

ΑΩ
A NEW HOPE IN LATIN AMERICA

Having nearly reached the end of this book, you may be wondering if there's any hope left for organized Protestantism. Let's review how we arrived at the situation facing us today.

When Martin Luther nailed The Ninety Five Theses to the church door in Wittenberg, Germany in 1517, it marked the beginning of an epic shift in the Christian world. European Christians left the Roman Catholic Church (RCC) in droves and discovered that they could forge a personal relationship with God. They were no longer bound by the elitism of the RCC, which hid the Bible deep inside its lavish cathedrals and sold salvation like baubles at the town fair.

Since that fateful day, the RCC and its private army, the Jesuit Order, have been waging war against the Reformers. The Jesuits not only succeeded in causing substantial harm to the Protestant Church, but have had a powerful impact on the education system, and on how Scripture is interpreted. They also orchestrated the rise of materialism, which interprets the universe as a soulless clockwork of celestial bodies. For 500 years, the Jesuits have steered science towards their goal of removing God from our world.

Protestant churches weakened under the strain of Jesuit infiltration and began to sacrifice doctrine for political correctness. They embraced ecumenism and some denominations formally reconciled with the RCC. By withdrawing their protest, they rendered the term Protestant meaningless. Some churches were compromised by external influences like the New Age movement, and most embraced destructive secular trends like feminism.

Surveying the Protestant world today, the statistics are disheartening. Protestant churches are losing members every year and total membership is dropping in most Western nations. According to Pew Research Center, Protestants represented 46.5% of all Americans in 2014, down from 51.13% in 2007.[1] In Germany, Protestants declined from 59% of the population in 1950 to 29% in 2010.[2]

Although the numbers look grim for North America and Europe, a positive trend is emerging in Latin America. At the turn of the century, this region had fewer than 200,000 Protestants. Today, the number has ballooned to more than 50 million.[3] Even after factoring in population growth (the total population of Latin America grew from 522 million in 2000 to 665 million in 2023)[4], the rate of conversion is so high that if the trend continues, Latin America will be predominantly Protestant before the end of the 21st century.

Latin America is a traditionally Catholic region. The Spanish and Portuguese who settled in the New World brought the Catholic Church with them and wasted no time in converting the natives. Over the centuries, Catholicism marinated in Latin American culture and took on a unique character.

Latin American Catholicism is easygoing yet fatalistic. It's associated with brass bands, family run restaurants, and an impending sense of doom. The church is the focal point of nearly every small town and usually its architectural highlight. But Latin Americans have always worn the mantle of Catholicism loosely, and now they're starting to shrug it off.

One possible reason for the dramatic change sweeping Latin America could be the perception that the Protestant faith is associated with individualism. As the multi-generational households that have long been a staple of Latin America downsize to accommodate shifting social trends, individualist ideals are replacing community-centric ones.

Protestant doctrine fits the new paradigm. This theory is supported by a recent Pew Research Center survey. Former Latin American Catholics who have converted to Protestantism were asked why they did so. Of the eight possible explanations, the most frequently cited was that they were looking for a more personal experience or relationship with God.[5]

"BE OF GOOD COURAGE, AND HE SHALL STRENGTHEN YOUR HEART, ALL YE THAT HOPE IN THE LORD." - PSALM 31:24

Protestant countries are generally perceived as more modern than their Catholic counterparts. In Europe, Protestant countries have the best trains, the most efficient courts, and the least corrupt police. This is not just coincidence.

German sociologist Max Weber (1864-1920) identified the link between Protestantism and the emergence of capitalism in his famous book *The Protestant Ethic and the Spirit of Capitalism*, published in 1904. Weber's mother was a devout Calvinist, so he was aware of the Calvinist belief in predestination. He posited that Calvinists, searching for clues as to whether or not they would be saved, pursued material success to determine if they were in God's favour. The importance of material success seems to have spread to other denominations as well, and so we have the phrase 'Protestant work ethic.' The phrase was undoubtedly inspired by Weber's book.[6]

Latin Americans have always looked to Protestant nations as ideals to aspire to. Perhaps they feel that adopting the religion of their role models will facilitate their aspirations.

The new Protestants of Latin America have been described as evangelicals. This term has many meanings, but the gist of it in this case is that Latin Americans abide by the Sola Scriptura philosophy that Martin Luther espoused half a millennium ago. This would suggest that they'll remain steadfast to doctrine rather than blindly following the destructive social trends that have derailed mainline churches.

What makes the shift to Protestantism in Latin America an even greater cause for optimism is the region's comparatively high birth rate. If Latin Americans continue to have children at the same rate as they have in the past, this will bode well for the future of the Protestant faith.

1. "America's Changing Religious Landscape." Pew Research Center, May 12, 2015, https://www.pewresearch.org/religion/2015/05/12/americas-changing-religious-landscape/
2. Evans, Jonathan. "Once a majority, Protestants now account for fewer than a third of Germans." Pew Research Center, February 12, 2019, https://www.pewresearch.org/short-reads/2019/02/12/once-

a-majority-protestants-now-account-for-fewer-than-a-third-of-germans/

3. Rodrigues, Richard. "Documentation: Losing Ground—As Catholicism Fails To Respond To Spiritual Needs, Latin Americans Are Embracing Evangelical Protestantism." Crisis Magazine, November 1, 1989, https://crisismagazine.com/vault/documentation-losing-ground

4. "Latin America and the Caribbean Population." Worldometer. https://www.worldometers.info/world-population/latin-america-and-the-caribbean-population/

5. Ashenden, Gavin. "The Rise of Protestantism in Latin America." Catholic Herald, December 12, 2022, https://catholicherald.co.uk/the-rise-of-protestantism-in-latin-america/

6. "The Protestant Ethic and the Spirit of Capitalism. Max Weber." Sparknotes. https://www.sparknotes.com/philosophy/protestantethic/summary/

ΑΩ
THE GIFT OF SOLA SCRIPTURA

Martin Luther accomplished many great things as he guided the Reformation through its formative years. He remained steadfast while enduring the wrath of the Roman Catholic Church (RCC) and held to his convictions despite facing great personal risk. Through his translations of Scripture, he spread the Word of God to vast numbers of Christians who had never seen the Bible before.

"A MAN'S GIFT MAKETH ROOM FOR HIM, AND BRINGETH HIM BEFORE GREAT MEN." - PROVERB 18:16

Luther's great accomplishment was cementing into place the precept of Sola Scriptura as the cornerstone of Protestant doctrine. In retrospect, it seems self evident that the Word of God should be the sole template on which to base one's faith as a Christian. God is truth, in stark contrast to the fallible words of men. Yet in Luther's time, the RCC had appointed itself as an authority on equal footing with God, revising the Fourth Commandment according to its whims and attempting to usurp God's role as arbiter of salvation. The Word of God was being corrupted.

Luther had the perspicacity to see that the RCC's teachings had strayed from Scripture, and that Christianity was in danger of being subverted beyond the point of no return. Moreover, he had the courage to act on his insights and push forward with the reforms that he knew were needed to save Christianity. We owe Luther an enormous debt of gratitude.

ΑΩ
UNLOCK THE WISDOM OF SCRIPTURE

Now that we've reviewed why the doctrine of Sola Scriptura is so vital to the Protestant faith, let's explore in detail what Scripture can do for us. The first step in using the Bible is learning to interpret it. Theologians have argued over how to do this for centuries, and have yet to reach a consensus. It's doubtful that they ever will.

The sheer amount of scholarly analysis directed at the Bible has had the unwelcome side effect of casting suspicion on its contents. When confronted with so many differing points of view about how to interpret Scripture, our natural reaction is to back off and keep it at arm's length until we're able to figure out which interpretation to believe. Sadly, many of us never complete this process. As a result, the Bible is relegated to that hard to reach shelf in the study with the other dust covered books we never read. Let's take the Bible off the shelf and look at it more closely.

The first step in understanding the Bible is to recognize the types of content it contains. The six commonly accepted categories of literary content in Scripture are History, Letters, Law, Gospel, Wisdom, and Prophecy. The first four (History, Letters, Law and Gospel) are historical in nature and are thus meant to be taken naturalistically (at face value). Only Wisdom and Prophecy are not meant to be read this way. Jason Lisle explains:

The vast bulk of the Bible falls under the literary categories of either History or Letters, and both genres employ a primarily literal use of language, which is the easiest to interpret. So, of the 66 books of the Bible, 43 are properly interpreted simply by taking the text at face value . . . In the New Testament, it's even easier; 26 of the 27 books are either historical or letters and are therefore primarily literal![1]

Many theologians have erroneously ascribed non-literal interpretations to historical sections of the Bible. This type of analysis is disingenuous. Only an analyst who wishes to discredit the Bible would argue that the historical events contained therein are not to be taken at face value. Jason Lisle gives a comprehensive classification of the books of the Bible by content type in his book *Understanding Genesis*.[2]

The second step in learning to understand the Bible is recognizing that most of us make an unconscious error when reading it. We allow our secular conditioning to act as a filter that determines what parts of Scripture we accept. In a previous chapter, we discussed the geocentric description of the earth in Scripture and how it clashes with the heliocentric view we've been indoctrinated to believe since childhood. We saw how this leads us to bend the meaning of Scripture so it conforms to our prior beliefs.

To take an example, we see in Genesis 1 that God created the earth before creating the sun and the moon. We know that Genesis is a historical book and is thus meant to be taken at face value. However, because we've been brainwashed into believing the big bang theory, which posits that the earth was created after the sun, we attempt to reinterpret Genesis so it conforms to our conditioning.

A related interpretive error is to treat the days in Genesis as much longer periods of time. Instead of reading a day as a 24 hour period, we reinterpret it as a unit of time that represents a thousand years or a million years. This is another attempt to reconcile the big bang theory with Scripture. This interpretation is easily disqualified. Each of the six days of Creation concludes with the phrase 'the evening and the morning,' signifying that they are 24 hour days.

If you're able to read the Bible without allowing your secular preconceptions to cloud your interpretation, then you've taken the first step towards understanding it. The next step is to unlock the wisdom within Scripture and apply it in your daily life.

Many parts of Scripture contain valuable insights of a general nature that can be helpful in times of difficulty. In my pocket Gideons International edition of the New Testament (KJV), the prologue provides the reader with a list of relevant passages to consult when feeling afraid, anxious, discouraged, etc.

This is a good way to get acquainted with the wisdom the Bible can offer, but there is much more available to those willing to make the effort. As we'll see in this chapter, Scripture can provide guidance on very specific issues, and studying it in detail can bring great rewards.

When the Covid-19 psyop was foisted upon us, we lost many of the civil liberties that we take for granted. Freedom of movement was severely curtailed, social gatherings were restricted or banned outright, and international travel became difficult or impossible. Everyone was faced with a very difficult decision: to accept or refuse an experimental vaccine that was being promoted as the only solution to a mysterious virus.

Many employers gave their staff an ultimatum: either take the injection or look for another job. By the same token, college and university students found that they could not continue their studies unless they complied with vaccination mandates. Faced with this extreme level of coercion, many felt they had no choice but to comply.

Before making an important decision, we seek out information that will help steer us in the right direction. We try to make an informed decision by researching the pros and cons of each alternative. But what if all the information we're relying on to make the decision is false?

Covid-19 began with a media blitz that assured us of the safety and efficacy of an experimental vaccine as the one and only solution. The recommendation to get vaccinated was unanimously supported by medical authorities, from your family doctor all the way up to the World Health Organization (WHO). This media bombardment created the illusion that we had all the required information to make a sound decision about whether or not to take the vaccine. However, when your ears are filled with the barking of a hundred dogs, it's hard to hear the meow of a solitary cat.

What many didn't realize is that all the information they were getting was coming from a single source: the WHO. The instruction to promote the vaccine was issued by the WHO to political leaders, health authorities, hospitals, and your family doctor. Few would have known that WHO management consists largely of former executives from the pharmaceutical industry. The WHO is essentially a bargaining agent for Big Pharma.

Opposing viewpoints were dealt with brutally. Doctors suggesting alternative treatments were vilified by the mainstream media and threatened with the loss of their licence to practice medicine. People from all walks of life who saw through the deception and defied vaccine and mask mandates were fined—or worse—for refusing to obey government dictates. No debate was permitted, and the public was left with one-sided talking points parroted by every mainstream news source on television, radio, print and the Internet.

Very few would have thought to turn to the Bible for guidance at the time, but those who did would have found something of great value within its pages. Turning to Revelation 18:23, we read the following:

And the light of a candle shall shine no more at all in thee; and the voice of the bridegroom and of the bride shall be heard no more at all in thee: for thy merchants were the great men of the earth; for by thy sorceries were all nations deceived.

The key to unlocking the message in this verse is understanding the word 'sorceries.' Sorcery in the contemporary context refers to black magic or witchcraft. Although the KJV New Testament is the most accurate English language translation of the Bible in existence, this is one case where it doesn't capture the nuances of the original Greek from which it was translated. This is one of those times where going back to the source language is essential.

Kudos to vlogger MrE for pointing out that the original Greek word from which 'sorceries' was translated is 'pharmakeia.' Does this word remind you of anything? Strong's Concordance defines pharmakeia as "the use of medicine, drugs or spells."[3]

MrE's conclusion is that Revelation 18:23 is a warning about the pharmaceutical cartel and the Covid-19 deception. The prophecy is incredibly precise, as it even foretells the worldwide scope of the event: all nations were deceived.[4]

The significance of Revelation 18:23 is something that the vast majority of Christians missed. Even if they had been alerted to the passage, they would have most likely ignored it.

Most Christians wouldn't think of questioning their government and the WHO. They would argue that medical science supercedes the Bible because science has progressed over the last several centuries. What they don't realize is that the Word of God is timeless. Scripture will never be outdated. God foresaw the advance of science just as He foresaw the crimes of the pharmaceutical cartel. Science cannot change anything that is in the Bible. It doesn't matter if the science dates from the Middle Ages, today, or a thousand years in the future.

Revelation 18:23 is but one example of the invaluable guidance that Scripture can provide. It stands to reason that there are many more passages in the Bible that can provide us with guidance at critical times, if we take the time to look. These gems of wisdom are beacons that can light the way as we navigate an ever darkening world.

The next time you're faced with the need to make a decision of critical importance, turn to the Bible. Treat it not only as a history book, but as a companion in your daily life. It contains boundless wisdom waiting to be tapped.

"AND JESUS ANSWERED AND SAID UNTO THEM, TAKE HEED THAT NO MAN DECEIVE YOU." - MATTHEW 24:4

We've been conditioned from birth to accept the pronouncements of our governments and secular institutions without question. The Bible can disabuse you of this conditioning. If you see a discrepancy between the Word of God and the messaging you see coming from the mainstream media, ask yourself which of the two you trust.

Tapping the wisdom of Scripture is not an easy task, but a lifelong journey. Perhaps God made Scripture intentionally opaque to train the faithful. The wisdom contained in the Bible requires a great deal of time and patience to unlock, but those who make the effort will reap the rewards.

1. Lisle, Dr. Jason. *Understanding Genesis*. Master Books, 2015, p.82.
2. Ibid, p.79.
3. "5331. pharmakeia." Bible Hub, https://biblehub.com/greek/5331.htm
4. "AND ALL NATIONS WERE DECEIVED BY YOUR PHARMAKEIA." Bitchute. https://www.bitchute.com/video/ilP0ClBCCzXb/

ΑΩ

NOW IS THE TIME TO PREPARE

Having come to the end of this book, you may be thinking about the various steps you can take to forge a stronger connection with God. As we've seen, this might include looking for alternatives to joining a church, familiarizing yourself more closely with the Bible, and delving into online and print resources to help you interpret Scripture. You may also be thinking about the amount of time that doing all this will take. This is usually the point where many people decide that they need to think it over a bit before jumping in.

Whatever you decide, keep in mind that too much procrastinating can have less than ideal consequences. We all need protection against what is transpiring in the world, and what is about to come. The Bible is our first, last and only defence against the decline that is currently taking place. The Word of God is our armour, our shield, and our sword. The tenet of Sola Scriptura is the great gift of Protestantism. It is the simple reminder that the Bible is the one infallible source we can turn to in order to hear the Word of God.

Just as a knight keeps his sword bright in readiness for battle, we too must prepare. We are faced with an imminent conflict in which it won't be possible to be a bystander and sit on the sidelines. Everyone will have to choose a side. Choosing the Christian way means preparing to fight as a Christian soldier. This doesn't mean fighting in the traditional sense, but by following the Word of God and obeying His will.

The prerequisite for becoming a good Christian soldier is gaining familiarity with Scripture. Just as the knight spends countless hours learning to use his weapons, so too must we study the Bible. Only by becoming intimately familiar with it will we be fully prepared.

Each of us may be called upon to do our individual part at the appointed time. It is important to have faith that God will guide us to take the appropriate actions. In the Book of Judges, God instructed Gideon to take only 300 men into battle against vastly superior forces. If Gideon had disobeyed this command, he would have surely been defeated. Only by trusting in God and following the instructions he was given, was he able to claim victory. The 300 men that Gideon took into battle were not randomly selected, but chosen by God. In the same way, God will command only those who are prepared to partake in battle.

The coming war I'm referring to is not a far off event. It has already started.

In the preceding chapters, we discussed the satanic inversion that is taking place all around us. Satan is the father of lies, and he increases his influence by coercing the weak willed—and those of weak faith—into denying God's truth.

Satanic inversion has permeated modern culture. Feminism is satanic inversion because it seeks to destroy the harmonious balance between male and female that God created. Modern art that pedestalizes the ugly, the wretched, and the defiled is another example. Instead of celebrating the truth and beauty that God bestowed on our world, it poisons our souls. The universal basic income initiative that is on the cusp of being rolled out in several Western countries is satanic inversion because it rewards idleness and destroys the individual's will to achieve. These are just a few examples.

Whenever you see something in the news that sets off an alarm in the back of your head—because you know that it wouldn't be happening in a sane world—you're witnessing satanic inversion. It's the feeling you would get if it's raining outside and the weather report tells you it's sunny.

Every instance of satanic inversion you're exposed to is a preliminary skirmish leading to the final battle. These skirmishes are designed to wear down our resistance until we lose sight of our own sense of truth and accept whatever we're told. It's a classic case of death by a thousand cuts. The plan is to leave us too bloodied and bruised to mount an effective defence when the battle goes into full swing.

You may believe that the decline of the West is purely accidental and that it can be attributed to incompetent politicians, greedy industrialists, and the other usual suspects. There is nothing accidental about it. It is happening by design.

Our world is caught in the grip of nothing less than an all out war of good against evil. This may sound extreme. Perhaps your sociology professor assured you, like mine did, that there is no such thing as evil. He liked to say that it is all subjective, and what is evil to one individual may appear good to someone else. Books like Hannah Arendt's *The Banality of Evil* perpetuate the fiction that good and evil are a matter of perspective, and that no person can be definitively labelled as one or the other.

Added to this is the even greater influence of film and television, where villains are often portrayed as comic book caricatures. From Flash Gordon's Ming the Merciless to Dr. Evil in *International Man of Mystery* (dir. Jay Roach, 1997) and its sequels, these caricatures parody evil. At the other extreme we have serious drama where the characters are clearly malevolent but are so over the top that we dismiss them as purely fictional. Hannibal Lecter from *The Silence of the Lambs* (dir. Jonathan Demme, 1991) is one example.

Then we have the clownish politicians who capriciously repurpose words so that we forget their true meaning. Former U.S. president George W. Bush liked to use the term 'axis of evil' when referring to Iran, Iraq and North Korea. This term has recently been called back into service by U.S. politicians to refer to Iran, Russia and China. As more countries wake up to the war crimes perpetrated by the U.S. against the rest of the world on a regular basis, the list will no doubt expand. 'Axis of evil' sounds like something out of a comic book, designed to scare children under the age of 10. At any rate, I have yet to see a dictionary that defines evil as a refusal to submit to U.S. hegemony.

The net effect of these secular influences is to plant the notion in our subconscious minds that evil in the biblical sense does not exist. And so we have the famous quote by Charles Baudelaire: "The greatest trick the Devil ever pulled was convincing the world he didn't exist." This trick continues to be pulled on us at every opportunity, and the Devil gets a great deal of help from pop culture.

Part of the reason Satan has been so successful in hiding his existence is that we tend to prefer comfort over truth. It would be very comfortable to live in a world without evil. Rather than acknowledging evil, it's easier to pretend that it simply doesn't exist. This explains the appeal of Renaissance philosophers such as Jean-Jacques Rousseau (1712-1778), whose quaint idea of the noble savage suggested that everyone is basically good.

We have become experts at cultivating a finely tuned capacity for self deception to avoid facing the fact that evil exists. When we read something truly horrific in the news, we find a way to interpret it so that it fits with our evil-free paradigm. We take great pains to delude ourselves rather than acknowledging that something evil actually took place.

Since so many people—Christians included—do not believe that evil exists, they are unable to recognize it when it appears. They have a false sense of security that makes them extremely vulnerable. This sense of security is no different than that of the delirious heroin addict who jumps off a tall building because he thinks he can fly.

The first step in protecting ourselves is accepting that evil is very much present in the world. Once we have done that, we can take the next step, which is doing everything we can to actively fight it. Sadly, very few Christians ever reach either of these stages.

It often takes a cataclysmic event to wake people up to the existence of evil. The turning point in my case was the Covid scamdemic. Everything about it, from the endless WHO lies to the lockstep response of every Western nation in depriving us of our civil liberties, reeked of evil orchestrated by a higher power. It was obvious that the preening sociopaths in public office were too dimwitted and incompetent to pull off something like this on their own. The only explanation was that they were operating under the direction of Satan and his generals, either consciously or in ignorance.

Each time Satan convinces someone to accept his lies over God's truth, he's a step closer to winning another soul. His goal is to reap as many souls as possible. Satan's soldiers—the Jesuits, aided by the Illuminati and the freemasons—have been promoting satanic inversion for hundreds of years. They've succeeded in removing God from the hearts and minds of many of His children and setting humanity on a path of self destruction.

The ultimate goal of this scheme is to bring about a series of events that will drastically reduce the global population and enslave the remaining survivors under a technocratic surveillance state that eliminates personal freedom and abolishes property ownership and reproductive rights. Couples, families, nations and religions will cease to exist. Individuals will be isolated, easily controlled drones with no sense of identity. They'll be denied access to nutritious foods, forcibly drugged and chipped, and will be dependent on pharmaceuticals to survive.

The process is already underway. The dozens of methodically planned and orchestrated wars of the past century—including WWI and WWII—and the more recent introduction of birth control, legalized abortion, and the Covid-19 psyop represent the initial phases of the depopulation agenda. More such events will follow.

Much of the mayhem that the globalists are orchestrating is targeted specifically at Christianity. Although the mainstream media will never mention it, Christians are the most persecuted religious group in the world. According to Open Doors, over 360 million Christians suffer severe persecution, including imprisonment, torture and death. This persecution will become more extreme as the end times draw near, as prophesied in Revelation 20:4:

. . . and I saw the souls of them that were beheaded for the witness of Jesus, and for the word of God, and which had not worshipped the beast . . .

The war on Christmas is being stepped up every year. Christmas is the celebration of the most important event in history: the birth of Jesus Christ. It is the time when we commemorate the arrival of our Saviour. Yet in recent decades, steps have been taken to take Christ out of Christmas and make us forget the meaning of the holiday.

This is being done through various ways. The first and most direct tactic is abolishing the word Christmas. Not long ago, Christmas greetings—both written and verbal—proclaimed 'Merry Christmas.' Now, the phrases 'Happy Holidays' and 'Season's Greetings' are used. Christmas cards that used to feature angels and Nativity scenes now show snowy winter landscapes. In the mainstream media, talk show hosts and journalists use strictly secular language. Any mainstream media personality daring to use the word 'Christmas' puts their job at risk.

Many Christians have been duped into believing that substituting 'Happy Holidays' for 'Merry Christmas' is merely a magnanimous gesture intended to make adherents of other faiths more comfortable at Christmas time. They're eager to engage in virtue signalling and show that they value inclusiveness and diversity. What they fail to realize is that erasing the phrase 'Merry Christmas' from our vocabulary is an attack on Christianity. Showing tolerance to others is a Christian gesture, but tolerance never involves compromising one's faith. Disrespecting our Saviour by referring to Christmas with euphemistic language is not tolerance, but compromise.

The second tactic in the war on Christmas is changing the meaning of the occasion by turning it into a generic winter holiday with no spiritual significance. The entertainment industry has been called into service to complete this task. Searching for Christmas music on YouTube doesn't turn up traditional hymns, but secular substitutes. Instead of "Silent Night" and "Hark the Herald Angels Sing," you're entreated to "Let It Snow" and "Jingle Bells." These songs have nothing to do with the birth of Jesus Christ.

The third tactic is commercializing Christmas. This is worse than simple consumerism—it is a direct affront to the teachings of Christ. All four gospels of the New Testament recount the story of Christ overturning the merchants' tables and expelling them from the temple. In the same way that these merchants desecrated a house of worship by turning it into a market, the retailers that turn Christmas into a sales event desecrate the memory of the birth of Christ.

Christians are taught to give selflessly, but how many of us actually do this? In most cases, we exchange rather than give. The rule of reciprocity is in full play, and some even go so far as to compare the costs of gifts given versus gifts received. When the exchange is not found to be equitable, a mental note is made to balance the books next Christmas. This is rather missing the point of what giving is all about.

The consumerism of Christmas was effectively critiqued in the animated television special *A Charlie Brown Christmas* (dir. Bill Melendez, 1965). In this poignant comedy, the hapless Charlie Brown laments the commercial hype surrounding Christmas and the selfishness of those around him, who are only interested in the presents under the Christmas tree. This feature, which was made six decades ago and carries an affirmation of the true meaning of Christmas, would never get the green light today. It has been scrubbed from YouTube, while more secular holiday classics like *Rudolph the Red-Nosed Reindeer* (dir. Larry Roemer, 1964) are still available on the platform. The latter is deemed acceptable by media executives because it doesn't mention Jesus Christ.

For those who commemorate the birth of Christ with pureness of heart, Christmas is much more than a remembrance. It has immense power—the power to bring peace and tranquillity to the most war torn places on earth. There are documented incidents from the front lines in WWI when ceasefires took place during Christmas 1914. In what became known as the Christmas Truce, officers and troops on several battlefields defied the orders of their superiors and laid down their arms. They sang Christmas carols and crossed enemy lines to indulge in camaraderie with their opponents, sharing cigarettes and drinks. For a short time, the insanity of war was paused. When we remember Christ, the will to do violence is purged from our hearts, and no longer has any claim to our destiny.

Easter is also under attack. The most blatant example of this was leveraging International Transgender Day of Visibility (TDOV), created by an American gay rights activist in 2009, to undermine the holiday. The date chosen for TDOV was March 31. This date was probably selected for its potential to coincide with Easter Sunday, which is precisely what happened in 2024.

U.S. president Joe Biden issued a proclamation recognizing TDOV in 2021. In 2024, when TDOV fell on Easter Sunday, Biden called on "all Americans to join us in lifting up the lives and voices of transgender people throughout our Nation and to work toward eliminating violence and discrimination based on gender identity."[1]

Transgenderism is an important tool in the satanist's toolbox. Transgenders mimic Baphomet, a demonic, goat-like entity which is frequently identified with Satan. It is a grotesque hybrid of genders with female breasts and male genitalia.[2]

The globalists who are pushing transgenderism honour Baphomet with every new transgender rights legislation that comes into effect. Sexually confused adolescents who are coerced into gender reassignment surgery by the state are unwitting pawns being served up as tributes to Baphomet.

Few realize how heinous a crime this is. According to a recent study published in The Journal of Urology, rates of attempted suicide among those who identified as transgender more than doubled after receiving a vaginoplasty (surgically turning a penis into a vagina).[3]

Individual liberties are slowly being eroded in every major nation. The right to own arms has already been eradicated from several European and Commonwealth countries. The U.S. will be next.

Access to meat, eggs and other nutritional staples is being curtailed through fabricated crises targeted at livestock farms. The excuses to kill cows and chickens range from fake disease outbreaks to climate change. In 2003, the Irish government started looking at plans to cull 200,000 cows to meet EU net zero emission requirements.[4] Many initiatives of this type are being implemented throughout the West. The motives are not hard to discern. People who eat nutritious foods to stay healthy are seen as obstacles to Big Pharma profits. Pharmaceutical companies want us undernourished and susceptible to disease, so they can make us dependent on medication.

The ability to control and preserve one's money has been under attack since the creation of central banking over a century ago. Central banks are a staple of communism, as detailed by Marx and Engels in *The Communist Manifesto*. Contrary to popular belief, central banks are not government institutions. They are consortiums of privately owned banks. They control the money supply of their host nation by creating money out of thin air and loaning it to the government at interest.

Most of us take it for granted that inflation is a fact of life that robs us of a few per cent of our purchasing power each year. However, it is not as endemic to the economy as one might think. Inflation is caused in large part by the endless money printing that central banks engage in. If central banks and their ability to meddle with the money supply were eliminated, economies would fare considerably better.

The next attack on wealth preservation will come in the form of Central Bank Digital Currency (CBDC) and the elimination of cash. CBDCs will give central banks the power to not only approve or deny every transaction you make, but also to attach an expiry date to your savings. If you don't spend your money by a given date, it will simply disappear from your account balance. CBDCs will regulate purchasing power using a social credit score. Say the wrong thing on Facebook and you won't be able to eat meat for three months.

The rollout of CBDCs is already in progress, supported by the global push towards electronic transactions. Sweden is one of the leading contestants in the race to go cashless, and many businesses in that country are no longer accepting cash. Other Western nations will follow suit.

Limited freedom of movement will be another key feature of the coming dystopia. The fifteen minute city, which the globalists advertise as a wonder of urban convenience, can be more accurately described as a soft prison. Special permission will be required to leave your designated zone. Until now, you only needed a passport to travel to another country. With the fifteen minute city, you'll need one to leave your neighbourhood.

We shouldn't fear what is to come or fall into despair. As Christians, we accept that evil exists, look it in the eye, and maintain a sense of hope and optimism. The Book of Revelation is an invaluable resource that can shed light on what is currently happening and what is about to come. We can take comfort in the fact that Scripture contains this critically important book to help guide us through the difficult times that have already started.

It's anyone's guess how close we are to the End Times, but it certainly feels like that period is fast approaching. Many theologians scoff at Revelation because it doesn't fall under the historical category of Bible books—but then how can it? It's part history and part prophecy. This doesn't reduce the value of Revelation, but increases it. Revelation is one of the most important books in the Bible, as it gives us a detailed look at what is to come. It is one of the most profoundly generous gifts of Scripture.

I've spent countless hours studying Revelation, reading various analyses about its contents, and watching videos that attempt to decode its imagery and symbolism. It's by far the most difficult book of the Bible to decipher, and I feel like I've barely begun to scratch the surface. As with all Scripture, there is only one correct interpretation, and that is the interpretation that God intended. The vast amount of disagreement over Revelation indicates that we aren't even close to fully understanding it.

"BLESSED IS HE THAT KEEPETH THE SAYINGS OF THE PROPHECY OF THIS BOOK." - REVELATION 22:7

One way of deciphering Revelation is to employ the classic theologian's approach of using Scripture to interpret Scripture. Revelation is closely tied to several books in both the Old and New Testaments, so studying the Bible from beginning to end is helpful. The astute reader will discover, for example, that Matthew 24 describes the same events that are in Revelation 6-8. This creates a bookend effect, since Matthew is the first book of the New Testament, and Revelation is the last.[5]

The mirroring between Matthew and Revelation is not only an example of the structural beauty of Scripture, but it demonstrates that Revelation cannot be dismissed as non-factual simply because it is a prophetic book. Matthew is a historical book—and is thus meant to be taken at face value—so the mirroring we see supports a naturalistic reading of Revelation.

It's important to keep in mind that Matthew and Revelation expressly refrain from revealing exactly when the prophesied events will come to pass. The countless YouTube videos predicting specific future dates for key events can therefore safely be ignored. In reference to the Second Coming, Matthew 24:36 tells us:

But of that day and hour knoweth no man, no, not the angels of heaven, but my Father only.

Having knowledge of this nature would be detrimental because it would resign us to a preordained fate. God gave us free will so that nothing in our lives would be preordained. If we knew the exact timing of what is to come, we'd have an excuse to stop whatever we're doing and simply wait to meet our fate. That is not what God intended.

Revelation serves not only to inform, but also to inspire. Although we may struggle to grasp all the wisdom contained within this enigmatic book, this in no way inhibits our ability to take inspiration from it. Part of our duty as Christians is to fight evil, stay strong, and never give up. Revelation gives us the inspiration we need to continue that fight.

1. "Conservatives clash with White House over Biden's recognition of Transgender Day of Visibility." PBS News Hour, March 31, 2024. https://www.pbs.org/newshour/politics/conservatives-clash-with-white-house-over-bidens-recognition-of-transgender-day-of-visibility
2. Wilson, Bob. *The Big Fake: How Killing the Sexes is Killing the West*. Self-published, 2021, p. 44.
3. "Attempted Suicide Rates More Than Double After Gender-Reassignment Surgery: Study." ZeroHedge, April 3, 2024. https://www.zerohedge.com/medical/attempted-suicide-rates-more-double-after-gender-reassignment-surgery-study
4. "Ireland moves to slaughter 200,000 cows over climate concerns." Human Events. https://humanevents.com/2023/06/03/ireland-moves-to-slaughter-200000-cows-over-climate-concerns
5. "Revelation Timeline Discovered." YouTube. https://www.youtube.com/watch?v=z3sciQ08T-c

ΑΩ
WRAPPING UP

Martin Luther did more than any historical figure since the Apostles to bring Christians closer to God. He had the perspicacity to see that the Catholic Church had gone astray and he had the courage to protest it. Luther liberated Christians from the notion that they needed a priest to communicate with God. He took the Bible out of the lavish cathedrals in which it was hidden and brought it into the light of day for all to see.

The Reformation was a major turning point in the history of Christianity. Millions of people gained access to the Bible for the first time and acquainted themselves firsthand with the Word of God. The publication of the King James Version of the Bible was one of the great achievements of the Reformation. Since its publication in 1611, the KJV Bible has been and will continue to be the definitive compilation of Scripture—the inerrant Word of God.

"BUT JESUS BEHELD THEM, AND SAID UNTO THEM, WITH MEN THIS IS IMPOSSIBLE; BUT WITH GOD ALL THINGS ARE POSSIBLE." - MATTHEW 19:26

The campaign that the Jesuits have waged against Protestantism for the last 500 years is a war against humanity. The Jesuits have infiltrated not only the Protestant Church, but the foundations of science, language and Scripture. They have done everything in their power to remove God from the hearts and minds of His children, employing satanic inversion to turn reality upside-down. They seek to convince us that evil is good and lies are truth.

Even though organized Protestantism—and the whole of organized Christianity—may be crippled beyond repair, Martin Luther's legacy remains. We are reminded through Luther's teachings that the Bible is all we need to live a Christian life, that each of us has the ability to forge a direct relationship with God through Jesus Christ, and that we are saved through faith, not works. These teachings are the essence of the Protestant faith. Though the path ahead may be dark and perilous, these simple truths serve to light our way.

Churches will wither, and the voices of technocrats, politicians and journalists will fill our ears with noise. None of this matters, because as long as we have the Word of God to guide us, we will prevail.

APPENDICES

APPENDIX 1: FILM RECOMMENDATION

It's extremely rare to find a film based on a historical figure that succeeds as drama and maintains historical accuracy at the same time. *Luther* (dir. Eric Till, 2003) is such a film. The German-American co-production treats its subject with care and respect. Joseph Fiennes gives a nuanced performance as Luther, conveying humbleness, sensitivity, and quiet strength in the lead role. This is how I would imagine the real Martin Luther to be.

There's a popular story template often used in books and films called the hero's journey. In this type of story, the protagonist is called to action by a mentor, initially turns down the challenge, and then accepts. He undergoes a metamorphosis, leaving his ordinary world behind to become a heroic warrior. By the end of the movie, the hero has vanquished his foe and earned the admiration of everyone around him. A classic example is *Star Wars Episode IV: A New Hope* (dir. George Lucas, 1977), in which Luke Skywalker leaves his past as an adopted farm hand behind and learns the ways of The Force to score a great victory against the evil Empire.

The appeal of the hero's journey lies in the development of the main character that takes place during the course of the film. The hero changes, evolving into a different person as the story unfolds. This is intensely satisfying to audiences, perhaps because it gives us hope that we too can become something greater than we are.

Martin Luther's journey was in every sense that of a hero. He started out as a confused youth who dropped out of law school. After becoming a monk, he transcended the limits of his station. Luther found the strength to stand up against the might of the Catholic Church and inspire those around him to join his noble cause, restoring the torn fabric of medieval Christianity.

The makers of *Luther* were blessed with a subject that fit the hero's journey template without the need for embellishment. The vast majority of movies with a religious theme take huge liberties with their subject matter to increase the entertainment value of the film. One example is *Noah* (dir. Darren Aronofsky, 2014), which unexpectedly enlists giants made of rock to defend Noah and build his ark. These giants are loosely based on the Watchers—fallen angels described in the Book of Enoch—but Enoch makes no mention of said angels transforming into rock creatures. *Noah* also adds several characters that don't appear at all in the Old Testament, including Tubal-Cain (the antagonist) and Na'el, a girl who Noah makes Ham leave behind as they flee from danger. The movie veers so far from Scripture that it should be regarded more as a fantasy inspired by the Story of Noah rather than a biblical film.

Luther, on the other hand, delivers a remarkably accurate depiction of the life of its titular character. The film captures a range of moods, from the sombre aftermath of a peasant's revolt to the lighthearted humour of a university lecture in which Luther calls out the hypocrisy of the Catholic Church. The film has emotional range but maintains tonal balance throughout, never descending into melodrama. Screen legend Peter Ustinov gives a memorable performance in a supporting role as Frederick III—his last role.

APPENDIX 2: ONLINE CONTENT RECOMMENDATIONS

Finding quality Christian content online, especially with a Protestant focus, is becoming increasingly difficult as the global media cartel steps up its war on Christianity. Many of the finest sites will not show up in most search engines.

Here are a few recommended sites featuring Christian content that were available at the time of writing. Most of these sites favour video over written content. Not all focus exclusively on Christian content:

Hugo Talks. https://hugotalks.substack.com/

Bible Flock Box. https://www.youtube.com/ @GregSereda

David Nikao Wilcoxson. https://www.youtube.com/ @EndTimesDeceptions

NicholasPOGM. https://www.youtube.com/ @NicholasPOGM

Apocalypse_Watchman by MrE. https:// www.bitchute.com/channel/OAx0XCP2TC4a/

1517: Christ for You. https://www.1517.org/

Dave Rebbettes. https://www.youtube.com/ @DaveRebbettes

Amazing Discoveries. https://amazingdiscoveries.org/

Truth Is Christ. https://truthischrist.com/

Stone Choir. https://stone-choir.com/

The Heidelblog. https://heidelblog.net/

Culture Wars. https://culturewars.com/

Street Church. https://www.streetchurch.ca/

GLOSSARY

Alphabet agency - Any of several U.S. government agencies commonly known by their abbreviated form (CIA, FBI, DHS, etc.)

Apocrypha - Works outside Scripture that inform some Christian religions

Artificial Intelligence - computer technology that simulates human intelligence and can be used for a variety of applications, ranging from problem solving to creating art

Autotheism - the idea that humans can acquire divine or supernatural powers

Charismatic Church - a church that values miracles and supernatural events, drawing on New Age concepts to concoct a belief system that incorporates elements of Buddhism, Hinduism, and Satanism

Current Thing - fictional crisis manufactured and promoted by the mainstream media to manipulate public opinion and foment inter-group conflict (examples include climate change, overpopulation, gender inequality, racism, etc.)

DEI - diversity, equity and inclusion

Freemasonry - secret society that originated in the 18th century and works in cooperation with the Jesuit Order to support Jesuit mandates

Globalism - international technocratic governance via a centralized supranational power structure, in which national governments no longer serve their people but act as enforcers of globalist policy

Illuminati - secret society that originated in Spain in the 15th century and works in cooperation with the Jesuit Order to support Jesuit mandates

Jesuit Order - private army of the Roman Catholic Church, tasked with destroying Protestantism and promoting Catholic dominance over organized Christianity

Mainstream media - global cartel of information and entertainment media organizations that control public opinion by promoting the Current Thing; members include the Big Six - GE, Newscorp, Disney, Viacom, Time Warner, CBS, plus Alphabet (which owns Google, YouTube and X), Meta (which owns Facebook, Instagram, WhatsApp), Wikipedia, and others

Pantheism - the idea that God, humans and nature are one

Psyop - abbreviation for psychological operation, in which governments and/or their agencies spread disinformation to manipulate public perceptions and attitudes, acting as a cover for achieving a hidden goal

RCC - Roman Catholic Church

Satanic inversion - the substitution of lies for the truth and evil for good, with the end goal of turning people away from God and towards Satan

SDA - Seventh-day Adventist

Sola Scriptura - Latin for scripture alone, Martin Luther's foundational precept of Protestant doctrine that recognizes Scripture as the sole and infallible Word of God and posits that all truth necessary to lead a Christian life is contained within it

Wokeism - dogmatic far left ideology advancing the destruction of the West by promoting gay rights, abortion, transhumanism, transgenderism, feminism, open immigration to Western nations, and DEI

ALSO BY BOB WILSON

The damage that feminism has done to Western society in the form of broken families and plummeting birth rates is now widely recognized. In hindsight, it's no surprise that any attempt to redefine the basic nature of male and female would result in disaster.

THE BIG FAKE:

HOW KILLING THE SEXES IS KILLING THE WEST

BOB WILSON

Feminism was never about equal rights. It was a premeditated plan to re-engineer the genders and weaken the male/female pair bond. Join Bob Wilson as he studies the changes in the West that reshaped the social contract between the sexes, and exposes the feminist movement as The Big Fake—a top-down psychological operation that was planned and executed at the highest levels.

Customer reviews

 4.4 out of 5

Made in the USA
Thornton, CO
06/23/24 22:50:50